THE HARMONY GUIDE TO
DECORATIVE NEEDLECRAFT

Lyric Books Limited

©1984 Lyric Books Limited
66B The Broadway, Mill Hill, London NW7 3TF, England

First Published in 1982
Reprinted 1993

ISBN 0 7111 0087 X

Printed in Belgium by
Proost International Book Production

Edited by
Kit Pyman and Carole Edwards

Text and samples by
Frances Healey, Doreen Holt, Nora Jones,
Diana Keay, Pat Phillpott, Kit Pyman and Pam Watt

CONTENTS

INTRODUCTION

Have you ever wanted to know how to make a beautiful patchwork quilt, how to smock a dress or stitch a tapestry cushion? Here is all the information you need to learn twelve different needlework techniques.

This introduction is concerned with the essential preliminaries to needlework — how to choose fabric and thread, what materials and equipment to buy, how to use a frame, enlarge and reduce designs and how to transfer them on to the fabric.

Each of the subjects in the five sections following has been written by an expert on that particular area of needlecraft technique, and gives you all the technique to begin straight away. Also included is a section dealing with those finishing touches which make all the difference to your work. How to press, stretch and mount your embroidery, and frame it to best advantage.

There are a large number of diagrams to explain the text and colour photographs of samples to illustrate different effects.

There are few things in this world more satisfying than the creation of a piece of original work, and if you have the right fabrics and threads and follow the careful instructions given here, you will achieve not only a beautiful piece of needlework, but the pleasures of a peaceful and creative hobby.

Materials

In order to achieve the best and most enduring results, it is important to obtain the best materials which you can afford and use the correct equipment. Details of all the special equipment and materials needed for each needlework technique are given within each section.

Fabrics

As a general rule, such natural fabrics as wool, cotton, linen and silk are the most suitable for embroidery, though a small proportion of man-made fibre will make the fabrics easier to care for. Buy the best you can afford, as good work deserves good materials. The following points may be helpful to you when you are choosing your fabric.

1 The fabric should be suitable for the purpose you have in mind. For example, fabric used for table mats should be washable and colourfast, and fabric for a chair seat should be strong and hard wearing.

2 Buy enough fabric to leave a good margin round the embroidered area. This will be needed for seams if it is to be a garment, for framing up if it has to be taut for the stitchery, and for pinning out if it has to be stretched. An extra piece for a sampler is very useful.

3 Choose the fabric to complement your design. If you are using a lot of stitchery, a plain smooth background would show it up, but if you are applying shapes in smooth materials like silk or leather then perhaps a textured fabric would make a more attractive contrast.

Threads

Threads for embroidery come in all sorts of fibres — wool, cotton, silk, linen and rayon, as well as many other man-made fibres. Choose a thread which suits your purpose and the technique you are using. Do not limit yourself to those threads specifically made for embroidery, you can also use materials supplied for knitting, crochet, weaving, macrame and lace-making, and unusual materials like synthetic raffia, ribbons, metal and plastic threads and leather thonging.

Equipment

A basic set of simple equipment is essential to good embroidery, and is a lasting pleasure to use. Have a case for your needles, a container for pins, and keep them together with your tape measure, chalk, pincushion and scissors in a portable box or basket. Threads can be collected in colour groups in a plastic bag, or skeins may be pinned to a piece of fabric in shade order and kept in a neat roll ready for use.

Thimble

A smooth strong thimble is usually worn on the middle finger of the working hand to push the needle through. Some workers use a finger shield on the index finger of the non-working hand when quilting.

Scissors

Ideally, three pairs are necessary. A small sharp pointed pair for embroidery, a long-bladed pair for cutting out, and an old pair for cutting card or paper.

Pins

Use fine sharp steel pins which will not mark the fabric, and are guaranteed not to rust.

Needles

It is important to have the right needle for the work in hand. Remember that a needle has to draw at least two threads through and must therefore make a hole big enough for them to pass easily without distorting the fabric. Only use a very fine needle with a single thread and very fine fabric. Needles come in a range of sizes, the higher the number the finer the needle, and the different types are listed below:

Beading A very fine long needle used for sewing on small beads.
Betweens A short sharp sewing needle with a small eye, often used for quilting.
Chenille A thick short sharp needle with a very large eye for thick threads and cords.
Crewel The most commonly used embroidery needle, with a sharp point and a long eye to take a number of threads at once.
Glovers A short strong needle with a triangular point for working with leather.
Sharps A medium length needle with a small eye for general sewing purposes.
Tapestry A blunt needle with a long eye, which is inserted between the threads of the fabric instead of piercing them. Used for counted thread, canvas work, and interlacing threads.

Frames

There are three basic kinds of frame, the ring frame (or embroidery hoop), the slate frame (which has straight sides) and the home-made frame which can be any size or shape required.

The ring frame This is used for working small areas by hand, and when doing free machine embroidery. A ring frame can be wood or metal, and consists of two rings which fit together. The inner ring should be covered with a crossway binding to prevent the embroidery slipping. The outer ring has a break in it and is held by a bolt and

The ring frame

Binding the inner ring

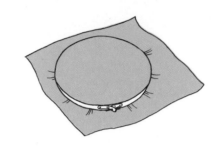
Fabric tensioned in frame

a tensioning screw. The fabric is laid over the inner ring, and the outer ring is pressed over this, gripping the fabric between the two. The fabric is gently pulled taut, and the tension screw is tightened to hold it in place.

For hand embroidery the ring frame is used with the stretched fabric surface uppermost, but it can, in fact, be used either way up. The right side of the fabric can be laid over or under the inner ring. For instance, it would be better to use the ring 'upside down' if you were stitching on small beads, to catch them while you work. Ring frames are always used 'upside down' on the sewing machine, so that the fabric lies flat on the working surface.

The slate frame This is a straight-sided frame made up of four separate pieces. The top and bottom bars have a strip of webbing nailed across them, to which the top and bottom of the work is sewn. The two side bars slot into the ends of the top and bottom bars, and are held with pegs, screws or split pins. The adjustment of these fasteners tensions the work. The sides are laced with fine string, or pinned with tape, as shown in the accompanying illustration.

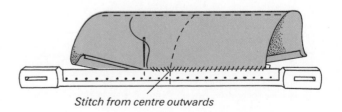
Stitch from centre outwards

The slate frame: stitching the fabric to the webbing

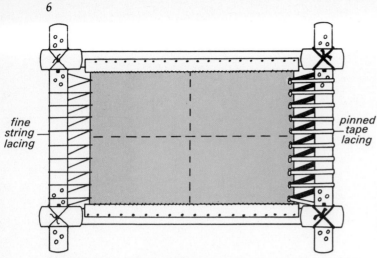

fine string lacing

pinned tape lacing

The slate frame: fabric stitched top and bottom and laced at the sides

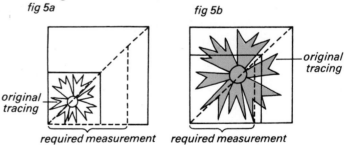
Completed corner

The home-made frame This could be a stretcher or an old picture frame, or four pieces of wood fastened together. The latter frame can be made exactly to fit the piece of work in hand. If you are

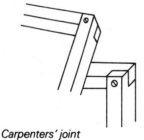

Picture frame corners

Straight pieces secured with angle iron

Carpenters' joint

Home-made frame construction

working a panel or collage, then the background fabric can be nailed or stapled to the frame and left in place. Start in the middle of each side and work outwards to each corner. The frame does not have to be beautiful as it will be covered, but the corners must be at right angles. In this way the finished panel will be already mounted.

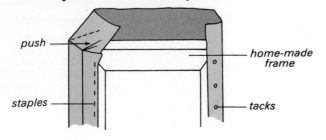
push

staples

home-made frame

tacks

Mounting fabric on a home-made frame

Designs

You may wish to use your own design, an illustration from a book, a postcard or a photograph. This will have to be scaled to the size of your embroidery, and then transferred on to the fabric.

Enlarging and Reducing Designs

Trace off the original design, and enclose it in a square or rectangle as desired.

To enlarge the design Place this tracing on the bottom left-hand corner of a sheet of paper large enough for the final design. Draw a diagonal line from the bottom left corner, over the tracing, and across the paper. Remove the original, and complete the diagonal. Draw out the base measurement horizontally from a point on this diagonal. From the far end drop a line vertically to meet the end of the base line. This gives both measurements of the required frame in exact proportion to the original.

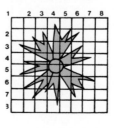

fig 5a

fig 5b

original tracing

original tracing

required measurement

required measurement

Enlarging a design

Reducing a design

To reduce the design Place the smaller piece of paper over the tracing and draw a diagonal across them both. Then proceed as above.

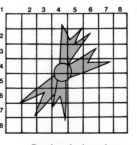

Original tracing divided into squares

Design being drawn out on larger grid

Divide both the tracing and the paper into an equal number of divisions (this is best achieved by folding and re-folding, and then ruling along the lines). Number the squares of both grids, starting from one corner.

Transfer the design square by square from one grid to the other. The more detailed the design, the more squares there should be.

Transferring the Design to the Fabric

Having drawn your design to the required size it can be transferred to the fabric in several different ways. Those methods which are used for particular embroidery techniques are described in the appropriate section, but a list of the usual methods is given below:-

Cut paper This is a template method for transferring simple shapes, and is useful for large outlines or repeating motifs. Trace off the design and cut out each separate shape. Pin these in place on the fabric and tack round. Different colours of thread can be used for different areas of the design. Alternatively, the templates can be outlined with an embroidery marker. Any marks remaining after the work has been completed can be removed by damping the fabric.

Transferring design with templates

Trace and tack This method is useful for fabrics (such as velvet) which will not take pencil or paint, as well as being a safe method of transferring a design without marking the fabric. First trace off the design on to tissue paper. Then pin the tissue in place on the taut fabric, and tack round all the outlines through both tissue and fabric. Use smaller stitches in detailed parts of the

Trace and tack method of transferring designs

fig 8

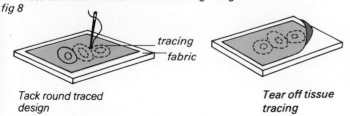

Tack round traced design

Tear off tissue tracing

design. When the design is complete, carefully tear away the tissue. If it does not come away easily, first score down the lines with a needle.

Prick and pounce This is a traditional and reliable method of transferring an elaborate design, but it is difficult to change the design later.
1 Draw out the design on firm tracing paper. Lay it face down on the ironing board and prick along all the lines every 2–3mm with a needle.
2 Lay the perforated tracing face up on the stretched fabric. Centre it along the grain and centre lines of the fabric. Pin in place.
3 Roll up a small piece of felt and tie it in the middle. Mix powdered french chalk with powdered charcoal (or blue and white tailors' chalk) to a shade that will show up on the fabric. Dip the roll in the powder and rub well over all the lines.
4 Lift off the tracing carefully, the design should be outlined in dotted lines of powder. Paint along the lines in watercolour with a fine, rather dry, brush. Blow off the powder.

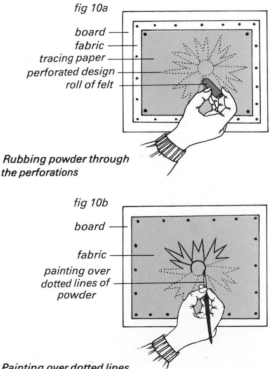

fig 10a

board
fabric
tracing paper
perforated design
roll of felt

Rubbing powder through the perforations

fig 10b

board

fabric
painting over dotted lines of powder

Painting over dotted lines

Dressmakers' carbon Follow the instructions for use making sure that the fabric you are using is suitable for this method.

Embroidery transfer pencils These are now available, and are supplied with detailed instructions. The design irons off giving a soft blue line. This may show on certain kinds of embroidery. Try a small area with your chosen fabric first.

STITCH LIBRARY

It is not necessary to know a great many stitches to start needlework, a few basic stitches can be used to make many different effects. This special section is designed as easy reference for a wide range of stitches. Instructions for specific embroidery stitches are also given separately within each section.

Stitches can be divided into four groups — flat, looped, knotted and raised. They can be combined into composite stitches, worked in lines, arranged to fill a space or scattered over an area. They can be worked formally to build up a pattern or a border, or worked freely, like painting, to make an effect of form, colour or texture.

Before starting work, group your fabric and threads to see how they look. Use a small piece of the fabric as a sampler and try out your selected stitches in different ways.

Suggestions for Working a Sampler

1 Choose the right needle for the fabric and thread (see page 5).
2 Use a fairly short thread in the needle, not more than 50cm (20in).
3 Experiment with the size and tension of the stitch. Small tight stitches will sink into the fabric, large loose stitches will lie on the surface.
4 Change the texture of a thread rather than the colour, i.e. use a shiny silk next to a matt wool.
5 Alter the direction of the stitch, — it will catch the light differently, which will change the colour or tone.

Listed below are the most widely-used embroidery stitches. Those that are used with a particular technique, such as Smocking or Canvas Work, will be found under that heading.

Stitches

Back stitch The needle is initially brought through at the arrow, and then a stitch is taken an equal distance behind and in front of the arrow as

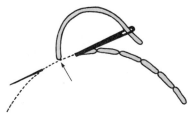

Back stitch

shown in the diagram. In the next stitch, the needle goes in at the arrow. A line of back stitch looks best in a fairly thick untwisted thread, and should lie in a smooth line.

Brick stitch This is a pattern formed by long and short satin stitches. The first row consists of regular long and short stitches, laid alternately, and subsequent rows consist of the long stitch only, laid between the stitches of the previous row. The last row is long and short stitches again. Brick stitch can be worked vertically, as shown, or horizontally.

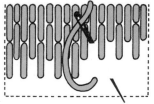

Brick stitch

Buttonhole stitch This is a most versatile stitch that can be used as an edging, a line, or a filling. Bring the thread through at the arrow, insert at upper point and take a straight stitch down, keeping the thread under the needle. Pull the thread through and repeat.

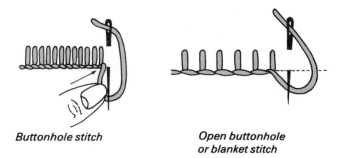

Buttonhole stitch

Open buttonhole or blanket stitch

Open buttonhole or blanket stitch Worked in the same way as above, except that a larger space is left between the upright stitches.

Spaced buttonhole stitch Groups of uprights are placed together, with a large space between.

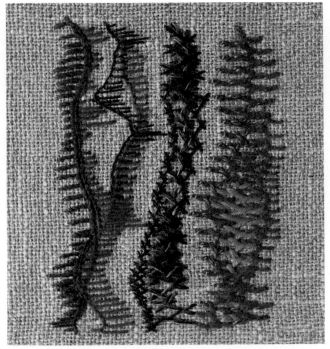

Buttonhole stitch; Herringbone stitch; Cretan stitch using Anchor Stranded Cotton, Anchor Pearl Cotton and Anchor Soft Embroidery.

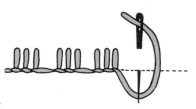

Spaced buttonhole stitch

Closed buttonhole stitch Two slanting stitches are worked, forming a triangle with the base line.

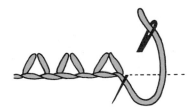

Closed bottonhole stitch

Bullion knot This stitch forms a tightly-wrapped bar lying on the surface of the fabric. Use a thick needle with an eye about the same size as the shaft, and a firm thread. Make a loose back stitch

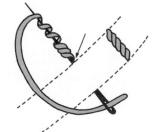

Bullion knot

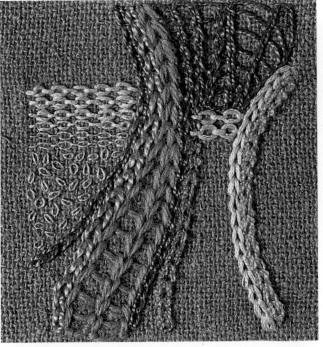

Chain stitch using Anchor Stranded Cotton, Anchor Pearl Cotton and Anchor Tapisserie Wool.

by bringing the needle out at the arrow, insert a short distance away, and bring out again at the arrow; pushing the needle most of the way through. Wrap the thread six or more times round this thick part of the needle, lay the thumb gently on the coils to keep them in place, and pull the needle through. Re-insert it at the original entry point, fixing the wrapped bar in position by tightening the thread. Some practice is needed to get the desired effect.

Chain stitch Chain has many variations, and in its simplest form is a good stitch for working curved lines. Come up at the arrow, take a stitch going down at the arrow and coming up on the line a short distance away. Keep the thread under the needle, and pull the needle through. Hold this loop down with the thumb until the next stitch is worked.

Chain stitch

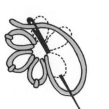

Detached chain

Detached chain A single chain stitch is made, and is secured by taking the thread over the loop and through the fabric. A useful stitch for a textured area or a scattered filling.

Cable chain Bring the thread through at the arrow and hold it down with the left thumb. Pass the needle under the thread from right to left and twist the point of the needle back over the thread towards you. Take a small stitch and pull the thread through.

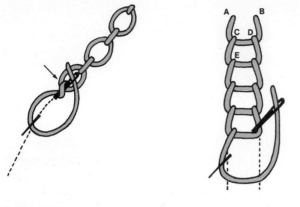

Cable chain   Open chain

Open chain Come up at A, then take a stitch from B to C keeping the thread under the needle. Keeping the loop loose, insert the needle at D within the loop and come out at E, with the thread under the needle. Continue in this way, taking slanting stitches from one side to the other.

Coral stitch This knot stitch is worked from right to left. Hold the thread along the line with the left thumb and take a small stitch under the line and the thread, and pull through, looping the working thread under the needle. The spacing of the knots can be varied as desired.

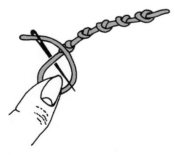

Coral stitch

Couching Lay a thread along the stitching line, and with another thread in the needle catch it down at intervals by taking a small stitch into the fabric. Thick and textured threads which will not pass easily through the fabric can be used in this way, couched down with a finer thread.

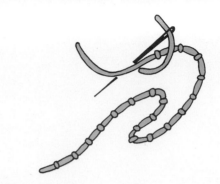

Couching

Cretan stitch Work from left to right, bring the needle up at the arrow and, with the thread to the right, take a small straight stitch downwards keeping the thread under the needle. Again with the thread to the right, take a stitch upwards, with the thread under the needle.

Cretan stitch

Eyelet stitch Make two small back stitches at a point on the circumference, both stitches passing in and out of the same hole in the fabric. Take two back stitches going in to the centre of the circle and out at the circumference. When working the second of these stitches, the needle should come out a little further along the circumference in readiness for the next two back stitches. If a fine thread is used and the stitches are pulled firmly, neat circles of characteristic 'eyelet' holes will be produced.

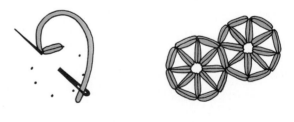

Eyelet stitch

Fly stitch Bring the needle through at A and, holding the thread down with the left thumb, insert it again at B, bringing it out again in the centre and a little below. Pull the needle through with the thread under the needle, and make a small vertical stitch over the loop. Fly stitches can be worked singly, or in rows.

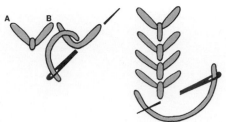

Fly stitch

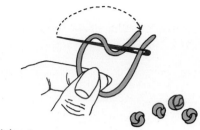

French knot

Feather stitch Bring the needle out at the arrow, hold the thread down with the left thumb, and insert the needle a little to the right, taking a small slanting stitch towards the centre and keeping the thread under the needle. Insert the needle again on the left side, and take a slanting stitch down towards the centre, keeping the thread under the needle point. Repeat both these two stitches alternately.

Double feather stitch Two stitches are taken to the right and left alternately.

Closed feather stitch This is worked in the same way as feather stitch, but with a straight side stitch, and produces a more solid line.

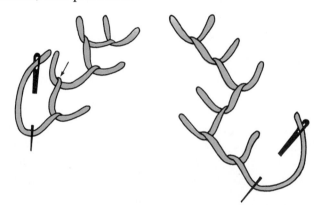

Feather stitch   *Double feather stitch*

Closed feather stitch

French knot Bring the thread through at the arrow and hold it between the left thumb and forefinger. Place the needle over and under the thread once, and twist the needle to insert it just above where the thread first emerged, holding the working thread firmly until it is finally pulled through. For a bigger knot, use two or more strands or a thicker thread. French knots are easier to work if the fabric is in a frame.

Hemstitch Hemstitch is worked over bundles of warp threads when several weft threads have been withdrawn, and makes a neat finish to a hem when worked alongside the folded edge. Withdraw the required number of threads and turn the hem to the edge of the drawn threads on the wrong side, tack in place. Bring the needle out at the arrow, and pass the thread from right to left under the first three strands of the ground fabric. Pull the thread through and insert the needle through a tiny section of the hem and the ground fabric. Continue in this way along the length of the border.

Hemstitch

Herringbone stitch This stitch is worked in a band between two guide lines. Bring the needle out at the arrow, and insert on the upper line a little to the right, taking a small stitch to the left with the thread below the needle. On the lower line, insert the needle a little to the right and take a small stitch to the left with the thread above the needle.

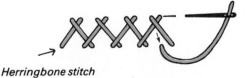

Herringbone stitch

Closed herringbone stitch Worked in the same way as herringbone stitch, with no spaces left between the stitches. This produces two neat lines of backstitching on the reverse.

Closed herringbone

Irregular herringbone stitch Both forms of herringbone stitch are useful for lines which vary in width, and with a little practice curves can also be worked.

Irregular closed herringbone

Needleweaving This can be worked on the warp threads of a fabric after the withdrawal of the weft threads, or can be worked on specially laid foundation threads as follows:- lay foundation threads as shown in the diagram, or as the design requires. With a new thread in the needle, come up at one end between two of the laid threads and weave over and under across the threads in both directions until they are covered. Do this with a blunt needle, the weaving does not enter the fabric except to come up at the beginning and go through to the back at the end to be fastened off.

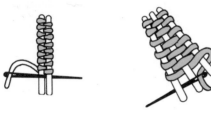

Needleweaving

Bullion knots; Couching; French knots using Anchor Stranded Cotton, Anchor Pearl Cotton, Anchor Soft Embroidery and Fancy Knitting Yarn.

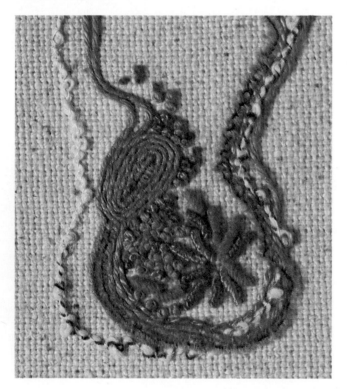

Running stitch Stitch along the design line making small stitches at regular intervals.

Running stitch

Laced running stitch

Laced running stitch Work a row of running stitches, then using another thread and a blunt tapestry needle, come up at the beginning of the line and weave the needle in and out of the stitches, without piercing the fabric.

Whipped running stitch Worked in the same way as laced running stitch, except that the needle slips under the stitches from top to bottom every time.

Whipped running stitch

Pattern darning This is a long running (or darning) stitch, worked in a regular pattern, in which a thread or two of the background fabric is picked up between each stitch. It can be worked horizontally or vertically, generally on evenweave fabric for accuracy of stitch length.

Patterned darning

Satin stitch Work straight stitches across the area to be filled, taking care to keep a good edge. The stitches should just touch each other and should not be too long. If a stranded thread is used, care must be taken that the threads are not twisted across the stitch.

Satin stitch lines Narrow lines can be worked as shown in the diagram. If a raised line is required, work a line of back stitching or lay a piece of wool or fine string and between the dotted lines, satin stitch over it.

 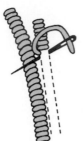

Satin stitch (worked to fill a space)   *Satin stitch (worked as a line)*

Satin stitch blocks Blocks of straight stitches can be used to form an all-over pattern as shown or worked at random to give areas of texture. In both cases, if a thread with a sheen is used, an interesting play of light occurs giving a chequerboard effect. This stitch is easiest to work on evenweave fabric.

Seeding Work small stitches of equal length placed at random over the area. They can be closely massed for a textured area or spaced out for a speckled effect.

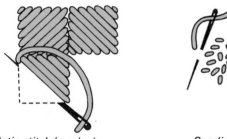

Satin stitch (worked in blocks)   *Seeding*

Sheaf filling stitch Work three vertical satin stitches of equal length. Bring the needle up at an angle under the middle thread, and pass the thread over and under the vertical stitches, and re-insert it under the sheaf. This can be worked in horizontal or vertical lines and can be used to fill an area.

Sheaf stitch This is a composite stitch which makes a thick raised band, and shows up best in a firm thread with a slight sheen. It is worked in four stages:-

1 Lay pairs of foundation stitch down the band at regular intervals.
2 Bring the thread through at the arrow, and working from right to left, wind it over two sets of foundation threads, until the width is comfortably filled. Move up to the next section, working this time from left to right, and slotting the threads in between those of the previous row.

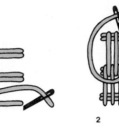 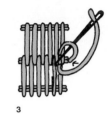
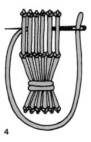

Sheaf stitch

3 Secure the threads at the intersections with a row of knots. Bring the needle up at the arrow, slip it under the two foundation threads from top to bottom. Pull the thread through gently and slip the needle under the last loop, tighten the knot. Work this knot stitch across all the intersections.

Hemstitch; Needle weaving; Pattern darning using Anchor Pearl Cotton.

4 Finally, work two satin stitches over all the threads midway between each knotted line. Make the satin stitches narrower than the band, so that the group of threads are pulled into the characteristic sheaf shape.

Split stitch This stitch is best worked in a frame in two movements, the needle coming up each time through the centre of the previous stitch. This makes a very exact line.

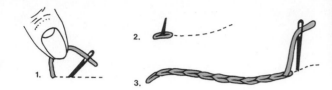

Split stitch

Star stitch A number of straight stitches are worked round a central hole. The needle must always come up at the circumference and go in at the centre. In the diagram, the needle is shown emerging for the next 'star'. A fairly thin thread should be used so that the stitches lie neatly around the central hole. On a firm fabric the central hole can be enlarged with a stiletto or a knitting needle to make the working easier.

Star stitch

Stem stitch Work from left to right taking small slanting stitches across the line of the design. Always keep the thread to the left of the previous stitch. If a thinner line is required, take the stitch from right to left along the design line. Stem can also be used as a filling stitch by placing the rows close together.

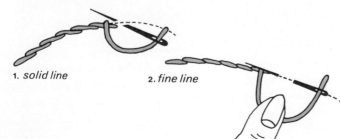

1. solid line *2. fine line*

Stem stitch

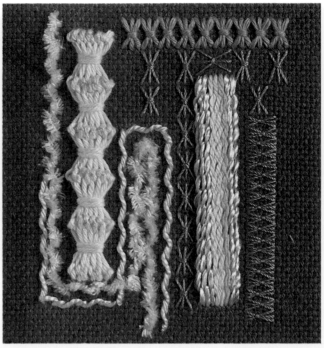

Sheaf stitch; Sheaf filling stitch; Stem band; Whipped running stitch using Anchor Pearl Cotton, Anchor Soft Embroidery and Fancy Knitting Yarn.

Whipped stem stitch If a heavier line is required, take another thread and work along the line slipping the needle over and under the stem stitch without entering the fabric.

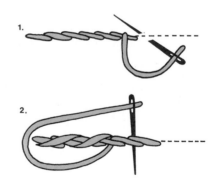

Whipped stem

Stem band Make a row of horizontal straight stitches at regular intervals along the line to be worked. Bring the needle out at the arrow and work a line of stem stitch on these stitches

Stem band

Wheels-woven and buttonhole; Star stitch; Eyelet stitch using Anchor Pearl Cotton and Anchor Tapisserie Wool.

without the needle entering the fabric until the end of the line is reached. Each subsequent row of stem stitch is worked in the same way, commencing at the bottom, and packing the rows close together so none of the horizontal stitches can be seen.

Vandyke stitch Bring the thread through at the arrow. Take a small horizontal stitch from right to left at A and insert the needle at B. Come up at C and pass the needle under the crossed threads at A from right to left without piercing the fabric and insert at D. Continue in this manner, maintaining an even tension so that the central plait is not distorted. The length of the side stitches can be varied and, with practice, curved lines can be worked.

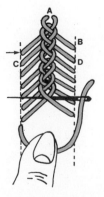

Vandyke stitch

Wheatear stitch Work the two slanting stitches shown at A and B on the diagram and bring the

needle up in the centre and a little below at C. Pass the needle under the two stitches without entering the fabric and re-insert at C. Continue as shown in the diagrams.

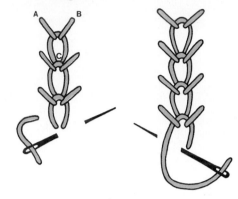

Wheatear stitch

Backstitched wheel Lay foundation threads as shown in the diagram, crossing at a central point, and fasten thread off securely at the back. With a new thread, and using a tapestry needle, come up between two of the spokes as near as possible to the centre. Working in an anti-clockwise direction and without piercing the fabric take the needle back over one thread and forward under two threads, working round until the spokes are covered. The number of spokes can be varied, and they can be laid in the manner described for star stitch.

Backstitched wheel

Woven wheel Lay foundation threads as shown in the diagram, crossing at a central point. With another thread, and using a tapestry needle, come up near the centre and weave round the circle under and over the foundation threads, until the spokes are covered. Threads laid in this way are always even in number. If laid as for star stitch, an uneven number can be laid, resulting in a different pattern of weaving.

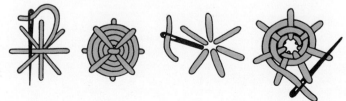

Woven wheels

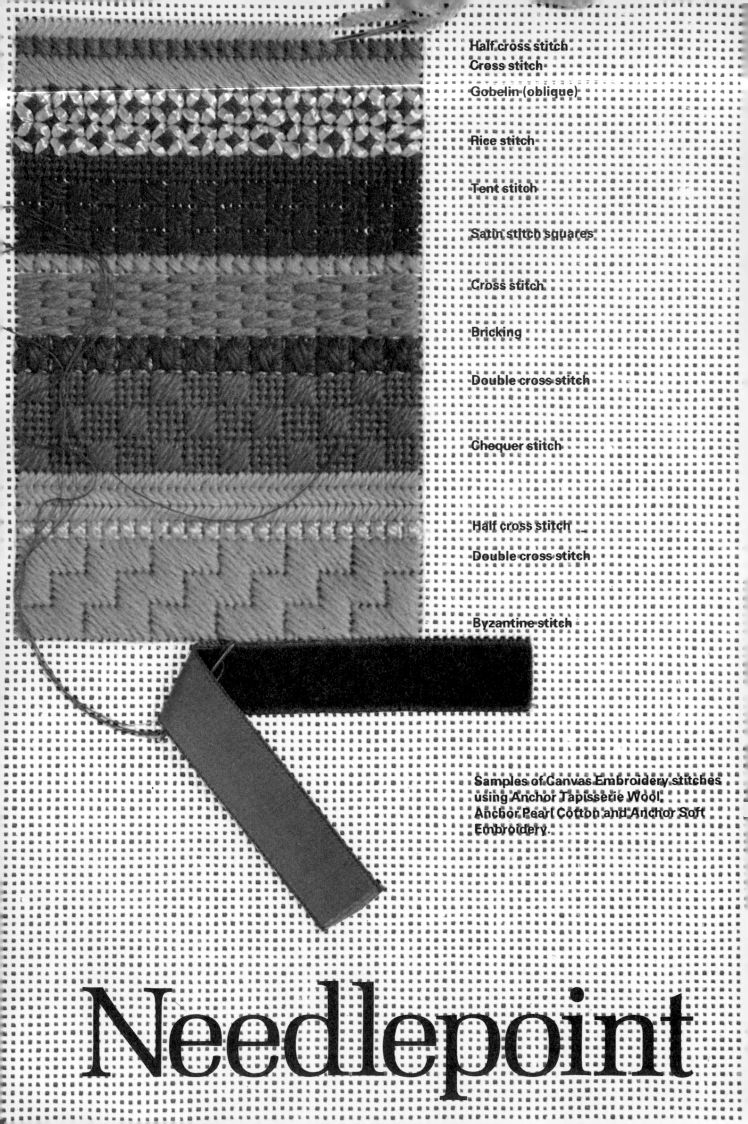

Half cross stitch
Cross stitch

Gobelin (oblique)

Rice stitch

Tent stitch

Satin stitch squares

Cross stitch

Bricking

Double cross stitch

Chequer stitch

Half cross stitch

Double cross stitch

Byzantine stitch

Samples of Canvas Embroidery stitches
using Anchor Tapisserie Wool,
Anchor Pearl Cotton and Anchor Soft
Embroidery.

Needlepoint

CANVAS WORK

Canvas work is embroidery worked on canvas, and the thread used is generally wool. Canvas work is often called 'tapestry', though real tapestry is woven on a loom and is not usually embroidered.

Canvas work is very strong and durable and can be used for soft furnishings such as chair seats, cushions, kneelers and even rugs. It is also used for accessories such as bags, belts and spectacle cases. Today it is also often used for panels or hangings, and for this purpose it is possible to use all kinds of threads, applied fabrics and raised stitchery which would be unsuitable for a practical article.

Canvas

Canvas comes in two main types, single and double thread. Choose a good quality canvas, especially for practical items. Use a fairly stiff canvas if you are working a small item in the hand without a frame.

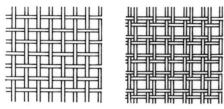

Single canvas   *Double canvas*

Single thread canvas This is recommended for beginners as you can use many different stitches on it. The mesh size is determined by the number of threads woven to 2.5cm (1in). For example, a mesh which has sixteen threads to the inch would be called a '16's' canvas.

Double thread canvas (Penelope) This is mostly used for cross stitch and heavier work, though the threads can be parted to enable finer work to be done. It is counted in pairs of thread to 2.5cm (1in).

Threads

Specially prepared wools can be bought for canvas work which are hardwearing, fast-dyed and mothproofed. They come in a large range of colours and different thicknesses. The threads should cover the canvas entirely, therefore they should be chosen to suit the size of the mesh. The closer the weave the smaller the holes and the finer the thread you will need to use.

Tapestry Wool (or Tapisserie) is a firm, well twisted yarn, moth resistant and colourfast. It is similar in texture to knitting wool and is available in a wide range of bright and subtle colours.

Crewel wool is a very fine wool which comes in skeins so that you can use as many thicknesses as you require. It is less easy to use than tapestry wool, but harder wearing and capable of being used for many different stitches. The range of colours is comprehensive.

Persian wool also comes stranded, three thicknesses being lightly skeined together, and it is slightly coarser than crewel wool. The range of colours is more limited and muted.

Other yarns include the whole range of knitting and embroidery and weaving yarns, including synthetic raffia and lurex threads if they suit your purpose. Any smooth thread can be used, and thinner threads are often useful for working over a thicker one, or filling in little gaps between stitches.

Hints on using and choosing threads

1 For a practical item, check that the thread is pure wool, mothproof, colourfast and thick enough to cover the canvas properly.
2 Make sure that the background wools come from the same dye bath, and buy enough to finish the work. As a very rough guide, one ounce of crewel wool will cover about 15cm (6in) square of 16's canvas in a plain flat stitch.
3 Keep subtle shades of one colour in their correct order. They can be pinned on a piece of fabric.
4 If the thread is too thin, use more strands, or use the tramming method on page 19.
5 Only use a short length in the needle, not more

than 50cm (20in) to prevent the wool ravelling.

6 Drop the needle at intervals and let the wool unravel.

7 Stretchy threads are difficult to use, and distort the canvas. Fluffy threads disguise the stitch. Dark colours show up a stitch less well than light ones.

Needles

Tapestry needles are specially made for this type of work. They have blunt ends which slip easily through the mesh. Choose a size which will pass comfortably through the canvas without distorting it, and which has an eye large enough to take your chosen threads.

Sizes 22, 20 or 18 would be right for the average 16 to 18 canvas. Sizes 16 to 13 are used for heavy double-double knitting wools and rug wools.

Preparation for Work

Use a large enough piece of canvas to leave at least 4cm (1½in) all round for stretching, mounting and framing.

Secure the raw edges with overcasting, zig zag stitch on a sewing machine, or covering with masking tape. Mark the central lines vertically and horizontally with a row of tacking. Frame up larger pieces in a slate or home-made square frame, as on page 6. Keep the selvedges at the sides, and fold the top and bottom over before sewing them to the webbing.

Covering edge of canvas with masking tape

Lay tape along edge   *Fold up other side*

Transferring Designs

Charted designs These are planned on graph paper and counted out on to the canvas. Use different symbols to represent different colours. The size of the finished design will vary according to the number of threads per inch of the canvas. To make a design to a particular measurement, lay the chosen canvas over the space, count the number of holes in each direction and mark the outline of a corresponding shape on your graph paper. Alternatively, if you have a design already charted that you wish to use, determine the finished size by finding the central hole in the canvas and on the chart, and counting the holes North,

South, East and West to determine the boundaries of the design. If the design is too small, use a larger size of canvas and vice versa.

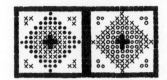

o Tan
■ Black
× Grey
□ White

Charted design

Traced designs Designs can be traced off on to the canvas itself. Prepare the canvas as described, frame it up if necessary. Draw the design on paper in a dark felt tip pen, and place the canvas over it. You should be able to see the design through the mesh. Using a fine *waterproof* felt tip pen (this is essential or the colour will run when the work is stretched), trace off the design on to the canvas. The outer edge, or any straight vertical or horizontal lines, should be drawn along a line of holes, as each stitch begins or ends in a line of holes. The design can be left as an outline, with colour notes marked in symbols or ends of wool tied in place. Alternatively, you can paint out the design on the canvas in colour with acrylic paints.

Method of Working

In the hand If your canvas is fairly large, roll up the ends (right side inside) and clip the rolls in place with pegs or pins while you work a small area. Stitch with methods 1 or 2 described below.

On the frame If the frame is not on a stand, it can be clamped to a table as shown. Keep it steady,

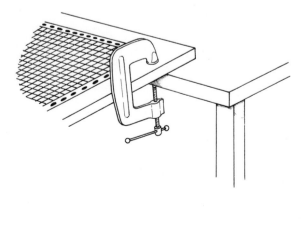

Canvas work on a frame

and work with your normal working hand underneath and the other one on top for maximum control and accuracy. Stitch with method 2 described below.

Method of Stitching

Method 1 Making a stitch in one movement. The needle is pushed down one hole and up through another, and then the whole length of thread is pulled through.

Method 2 Making a stitch in two movements. The needle is pushed down through one hole, pulled through to the other side, then pushed up through the next hole. The tightening of the thread need only be done when the thread is pulled through to the right side. This is a quick and neat method and generally produces better results than Method 1.

Tramming

Tramming is a method of thickening up the work by laying threads across the weft of the canvas and then stitching over them. Tramming can be done either as the work progresses or laid beforehand. In the latter case the threads are in the colours of the design and act as a guide. Some tapestry kits are already trammed.

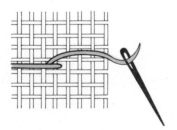

Tramming

Hints on Stitching

Start by making a knot at the end of the wool, and running it through several meshes, then working back over them. Leave the knot on the front, and cut it off when work is complete. Finish off at the back by darning the thread through the back of the work.

Where possible, bring the needle up from the wrong side into an empty hole and go down in a filled hole (made by previous stitch). This ensures that any little bits of fluff are pulled through to the wrong side, and a neat 'dimple' is made between stitches on the right side. Horizontal or vertical stitches need thicker thread than diagonal stitches which have to cover less canvas threads.

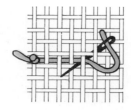

Starting

When working a multicoloured design, it saves a lot of finishing off at the back if the wool is brought through to the front and laid aside until the colour is needed again in that area.

When counting to see if a stitch will fit, count the holes rather than the threads. Remember a square that uses five holes will always use the last hole of the previous square.

Stitches

The most popular type of canvas work today uses Tent Stitch throughout, otherwise known as Gros Point if used on double thread canvas and Petit Point if used on single thread canvas. Most of the canvas work kits on sale are designed to be worked in this way.

There are, however, a great number of canvas work stitches, and we have listed below some of the most useful and interesting ones.

If you would like to practise the stitches, we have designed a sampler using ten of them. The sampler can be worked either as a rectangle or as a square, and can be made up afterwards into a useful item like a bag or a cushion.

You will need a piece of single canvas, 13 threads to the 2.5cm (1in). The rectangular sampler measures approximately 9cm × 14cm (3½in × 5½in), and the other one is about 13cm (5in) square, so add the required margin according to the article you are going to make. Use scraps of soft Embroidery, Tapisserie wools and perhaps the odd length of synthetic raffia or Pearl cotton (to add shine on crossed corners, for instances).

Plan your colour scheme before you begin. You can make a rough plan by sticking bits of the threads you plan to use in the right order on a piece of paper.

When working the square, you may find that your chosen stitch will not fit exactly the number of holes that have to be filled. In this case start each line from the corners and work towards the centre. If there is not room for a whole stitch in the middle, work part of one. Work the diagonal satin stitches pointing inwards from each corner.

Square sampler using Anchor Tapisserie Wool and Anchor Pearl Cotton.

Key to square sampler
1) Satin stitch
2) Half cross stitch
3) Rice stitch
4) Tent stitch
5) Cross stitch
6) Double cross with crossed corners
7) Long armed cross
8) Chequer stitch

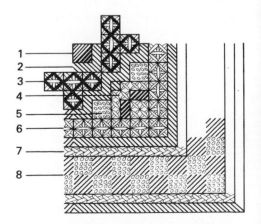

To make the finished sampler bigger, you can stitch velvet ribbon on to the canvas by hand using stab stitch. Work down the line of holes last used for the previous stitch. Another way of increasing the size is to set the canvas work in a piece of log cabin patchwork.

Brick stitch This is a useful shading stitch, or for making a solid filling. It is worked in rows alternately from left to right and right to left. The first row is long and short stitches — subsequent rows are of satin stitches of even length fitted in 'brick' formation.

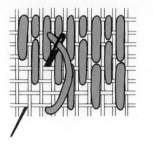

Brick stitch

Byzantine stitch Byzantine stitch is always worked on the exact diagonal. The basic unit is four satin stitches worked diagonally over four vertical and four horizontal threads of the canvas, which are arranged in 'steps' as shown. You can alter the number of threads over which it is worked, and the direction of the 'steps'.

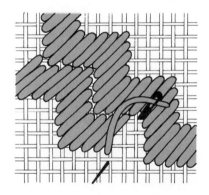

Byzantine stitch

Chequer stitch This stitch is worked on the diagonal in a pattern of squares, each square covers three, four or five vertical and horizontal threads of the canvas. The first square is filled with small stitches, each one over a vertical thread, and the second with graduated stitches, and the squares are arranged alternately. It is

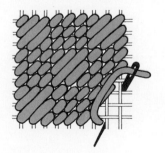

Chequer stitch

easiest to work diagonally, from one square of tiny stitches to the next, and then go back to the top again and work the longer stitches.

Cross stitch This stitch is sometimes called gros point. It is usually worked over two vertical and two horizontal threads of the canvas. The first row can be worked with a single diagonal from right to left, and the stitches 'crossed' in a row from left to right. Make sure the top thread lies in the same direction throughout the work. Half cross stitch is a diagonal stitch over two horizontal and two vertical threads.

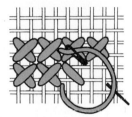

Cross stitch

Cross stitch — Crossed corners, see Rice stitch

Cross stitch (double) Sometimes called Leviathan stitch or Smyrna stitch, this is a diagonal cross stitch, covered with an upright one. The order of working is shown by the numbers on the diagram. If the crosses are worked in the reverse order, the effect is quite different. The crosses can be worked in different colours.

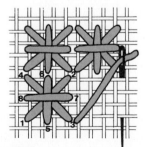

Cross stitch (double)

Cross stitch (long-armed) It is also called plaited slav stitch. It is a good stitch for borders and edgings. It can be worked on the fold to make a neat edge to an article, by working over two and four threads, or three and five holes.

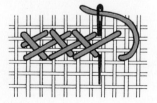

Long armed cross stitch

Left: Brick stitch; centre: Flecked Bricking; right: Free Gobe... blocks) using Anchor Tapisserie Wool, Anchor Stranded Cotton, Soft Embroidery.

Diagonal stitch Satin stitches worked over two, three, four, three and two horizontal and vertical threads of canvas, in diagonal rows from top left to bottom right. The longest stitches of one row lie diagonally below the shortest stitch of the row above.

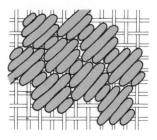

Diagonal stitch

Gobelin stitch Also known as oblique gobelin stitch or gros point. This is a slanting satin stitch worked over two horizontal threads and one vertical thread of the canvas. It is an elongated tent stitch, originally intended to simulate tapestry weaving, and is worked in the same way, one row from right to left, followed by one row from left to right.

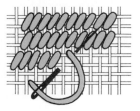

Gobelin stitch (oblique)

Gobelin stitch (encroaching) The stitches are longer than gobelin stitch, being worked over four or five horizontal canvas threads and slanted diagonally over one vertical thread. Each row overlaps the last by one thread of canvas.

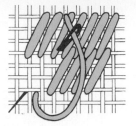

Gobelin stitch (encroaching)

Gobelin stitch (upright) This can be worked over any number of threads, but a thicker yarn will be needed as this stitch follows the weave of the canvas. If the result is thin, tramming may be necessary. Never pull this stitch tightly.

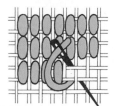

Gobelin stitch (upright)

Hungarian stitch This stitch is called mosaic stitch if it is worked diagonally. Groups of three upright stitches are worked over two, four and two horizontal threads. Leave two vertical threads between each group, and fit the second row. It can be worked in one colour, or in two as shown.

Hungarian stitch

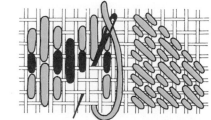

Worked vertically   *Worked diagonally (mosaic stitch)*

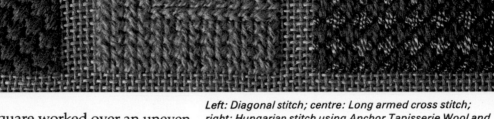

Norwich stitch A square worked over an uneven number of threads. The larger it is the better it looks. Use a long length of yarn, and work as shown. All stitches on the back should follow the outer line of holes. Follow the numbering until the last stitch, when the needle should be slipped *under* instead of over the stitch 29–30, before entering the canvas at hole 36.

Left: Diagonal stitch; centre: Long armed cross stitch; right: Hungarian stitch using Anchor Tapisserie Wool and Anchor Pearl Cotton.

is completed, *repeat the first stitch*, as it gives a better diagonal on top.

Norwich stitch

Rhodes stitch

Rice stitch This is often worked with thick yarn for the large crosses, and finer yarn for the small crossing stitches. Start by working the large cross stitches over four vertical and four horizontal threads of the canvas, then cross the corners in a finer thread, following the numbering shown.

Scottish squares These consist of squares of slanting graduated stitches, outlined with small stitches worked over a single intersection of canvas threads. Work the outline stitches first.

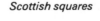

Scottish squares

Rice stitch

Rhodes stitch This can be worked over a square or a rectangle. Bring the needle out at 1, insert at 1b, bring it out at 2, insert at 2b and so on, following the direction of the arrows. When the square

Tent stitch Also called petit point, it is used for fine work, on single thread canvas only, it is a slanting stitch taken over one intersection of canvas threads. For small areas use the horizontal method as shown. For large areas use the diagonal method as shown. Note that on the way down the needle goes in vertically, and on the way up it goes in horizontally. Always go down into the gaps between the previous row of stitches. The diagonal method does not distort the canvas as much as the horizontal method.

Velvet stitch This stitch makes a looped pile. It may be trimmed to form a close-cut pile, in which case a thick yarn or rug wool should be used. Come up at 1 and go over two intersections and go down at 2. Come up at 1 again, and go down into 2 leaving a loop of thread hanging. Come up at 3, and complete the cross by going down at 4. Come out at 3 again for the next stitch.

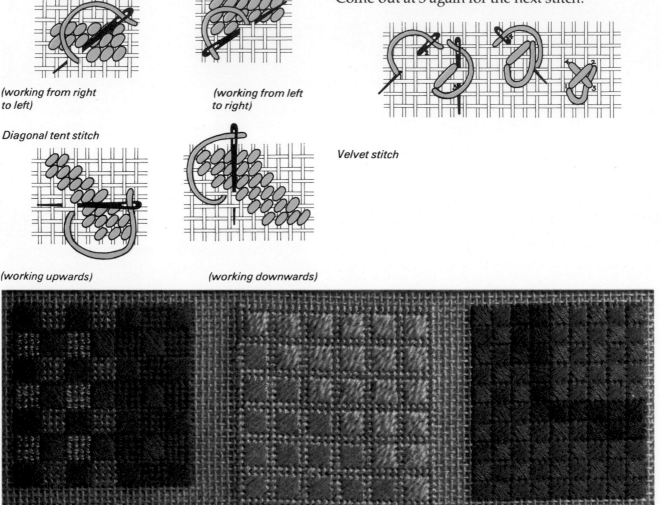

Horizontal tent stitch

(working from right to left)

(working from left to right)

Diagonal tent stitch

(working upwards)

(working downwards)

Velvet stitch

Left: Alternating Chequer stitch; centre: Scottish stitch; right: Flat stitch (Satin squares) using Anchor Stranded Cotton and Anchor Pearl Cotton.

Left: Norwich stitch; centre: Velvet stitch; right: Rhodes stitch using Anchor Tapisserie Wool and fancy yarn.

FLORENTINE

Florentine work is also known as *bargello* because there are some fine examples in the Bargello museum in Florence. The basic stitch is simple, a straight stitch, and the patterns vary from very easy to the more complicated designs. Some varieties of florentine work travel in flame-like leaps over the canvas, giving rise to a third name, flame stitch.

Canvas

Single canvases are the most suitable for Florentine work. The double canvases are not suitable as the wool will not cover the threads. Raffia canvas is the coarsest with 10 holes to 2.5cm (1in). This can be used with thick wools, even 2 ply rug wool, for cushions on a bold scale, or for tote bags or rugs. The medium canvases are 12, 14 and 16 holes to 2.5cm (1in) and these can be worked with the more usual wools. 18 threads per 2.5cm is suitable for people with good eyesight and even finer canvases can be bought for small pieces of work.

Buy the best quality canvas for anything which is to last and wear well. Cheaper canvases are suitable for pieces which are decorative, but avoid any with harsh dressing (stiffening) which will wear the working threads and be a false economy.

Always allow a good margin round the work. A minimum of 4cm (1½in) is suggested to allow for making up. When the canvas is cut out, secure the edges as suggested on page 18.

Run a tacking thread through the centre of the canvas in both directions, this makes a check point when working. Begin in the centre of the pattern.

Using Other Fabrics

Evenweave, or near evenweave fabrics can be used for Florentine work. Embroidery shops sell linens and cottons which are even, but near evenweave fabrics may be found in dress and furnishing departments which are suitable for all except four-way bargello. This will be distorted on any but completely evenweave material.

When using these fabrics, it is not necessary to work the entire surface and some rows may be left unworked. This is useful if you want to use some Florentine work on a jacket or dress.

Threads

Florentine work may be done in one type of thread only, nowadays usually wool. Silk was often used in the past, sometimes for details in the design. If you are making something which will not have to take much wear, you may like to include mercerised cotton threads to give an occasional glint.

Crewel wools are stranded and the number of strands in the needle may be adjusted to suit the size of the canvas. The colours are mostly soft, being inspired by traditional embroidery designs, and they are produced in wide shade and tonal ranges. This means that you can buy one colour in several tones from dark to light. Some of the shades are very close, so keep them organised if you are working by artificial light. You can safety-pin each skein to a piece of an old sheet in tonal order. When choosing colours, do not think that you *must* have all tones of one colour. For example, if your main green is sage, you may find that a pale shade of a more yellowy-green will look better in the lighter tones. It may produce a livelier effect.

Persian wools are slightly thicker, but these too may be used with more than one strand in the

Right: Simple Florentine stitch design using Anchor Tapisserie Wool.

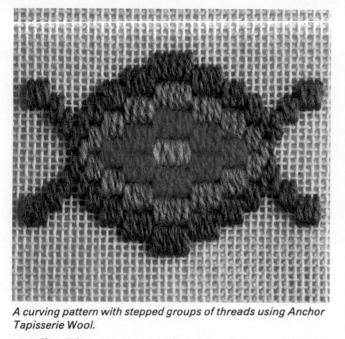

A curving pattern with stepped groups of threads using Anchor Tapisserie Wool.

needle. There are more bright colours available, though the range of tones from light to dark is not as wide as in crewel wools.

Other wools may be used if wearing quality is unimportant. Tapestry wools are soft and look very well in Florentine work. On coarse canvas, knitting and crochet yarns can be used. Some embroidery or weaving threads will give special effects.

If you are working a large piece, make sure that you have enough wool to complete the work as dye lots vary in colour.

Needles

Tapestry needles are used, as for other canvas work, as described on page 18.

Frames

Frames need not be used for Florentine work, but for those who like working on frames there is no reason why they should not be used, square or rectangular ones are suitable. Do not use the ring or tambour frames as they will distort the canvas.

Fastening On and Off

Begin with a tail of wool left on the surface of the work. This can be darned into the back when the needle-full is used up and finishing off is done in the same way. You will find that certain areas of some patterns have very long stitches on the back which will not provide a secure fastening, so always make sure that you leave sufficient wool to reach a part of the pattern where fastening on or off will not slip out.

Simple Patterns

Try out some patterns first so that you understand how they work before working from a chart. You may like to make a sampler or you may prefer to make some small easy pieces such as pincushions or needlebooks. The simplest patterns use the same length of stitch all the time and the 'steps' by which the stitches move up and down the canvas are also the same.

Begin with a simple zigzag. Take a length of dark wool. Rather longer pieces of wool may be used for Florentine than for other forms of canvas work because there is not so much wear as the wool passes through the canvas. Never work with too long a length, however, or you will waste time hauling it through the canvas. Experience will show you how much to use, 51–56cm (20in–22in) is suggested.

The first stitch passes over four horizontal threads of canvas and the needle comes out in the next row of holes but two threads up. Work as in the diagram across the canvas. Start the next row four threads above the first row with a shade lighter wool and work in the same way across the canvas, the needle coming down into the hole occupied by the previous stitch.

This simple pattern can be varied by the choice of colour. If you choose several tones of the same colour, you will get a quiet watery effect. If you work from dark to light, then dark to light again the pattern will be more marked than if you go from dark to light and then through medium back to dark. The depth of the pattern will appear greater. Try this out, then try introducing a second colour.

Now try reversing the pattern, as in the diagram. The top stitch of one dark row acts in place of the bottom stitch of the other dark row and a diamond is formed, as shown in the sample.

Now try working more than one stitch at the same level and you will have a gentler zigzag.

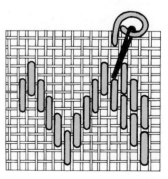

First row *Second row*

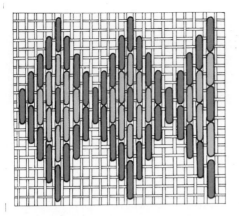

Reversing the pattern

Curving patterns These are made by varying the number of stitches in the blocks as the diagram shows.

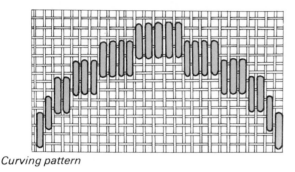

Curving pattern

Saving Wool

It is possible to work Florentine in a slightly different way to economise in wool on the back of the work. The needle makes the shortest journey from stitch to stitch on the back of the work. This does not always make such a neat effect, because

Four-way Bargello starting from a single thread in each direction using Anchor Tapisserie Wool.

Four-way Bargello starting from a central motif using Anchor Tapisserie Wool.

the 'pull' of the stitch is altered and it will be slightly askew instead of lying straight with the canvas. It is not recommended for use on pieces like chair seats where the wool on the back of the work in the usual method helps to make the embroidery last longer.

Four-Way Bargello

Square cushions or bags can be worked in this way. The pattern begins at the centre and is worked outwards, north, south, east and west.

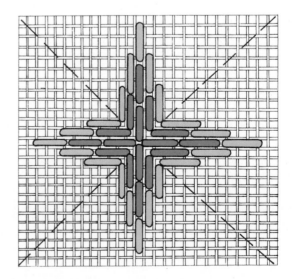

Four-way bargello

The rows fit into each other on the diagonals. Take care not to pull very short stitches at the diagonal too tight or the wool will not fill the canvas.

Embroidery

CREWEL WORK

Crewel work takes its name from the crewel wools with which it is embroidered. Designs are bold, the soft wool is pleasant to handle and the work is quick to do. It has always been used for furnishings and a cushion or a work bag would be ideal to begin with.

Fabrics

A naturally-coloured twill-weave linen or linen and cotton is woven specially for this work and can be bought at good needlework shops. It is expensive and there are several alternatives. The best fabrics for crewel work are of medium to heavy weight which are pleasant to handle. You can get an idea of the required effect by trying some of the stitches on pieces from your bit bag. These can vary from coarse cottons, furnishing fabrics, to dress or suiting woollens.

Avoid harsh fabrics; these will wear the wool as you stitch. Loosely woven fabrics will not give good results with some of the stitches.

Yarns

Crewel wools are fine, slightly twisted wools which can be bought at specialist embroidery or craft shops. They are made in a wide range of colours and each colour has several shades from pale to dark. The wool can be bought in small skeins or larger hanks. To begin with, buy a few skeins in colours which you like.

Persian yarns are thicker than the crewel wools though, like them, they are also slightly twisted and so easy to use. The colour range is not so large and shades of each colour are fewer. There are some brighter colours in Persian yarn than in crewel wool and this may influence your choice as well as the speed of working with a thicker wool.

Crewel and Persian wools are both made to wear reasonably well and this is important for anything you make which has to stand up to wear. For hangings and pictures, this is less important and other wools can be introduced.

Tapestry wools are thick and soft, but care must be taken in stitching with them. Never use too long a length in the needle or the wool will fray where it passes through the eye.

Knitting and some weaving wools can be used. On very large, coarse pieces, 2-ply rug wool can be used. It can be bought cheaply as long *thrums*, the ends which are cut off the carpet looms. (Do not buy short or unsorted thrums because the short pieces are only suitable for hooked rugs.)

Needles

Crewel needles have long eyes and sharp points. A packet of mixed sizes will provide for all thicknesses of wool except the coarsest. Use the larger chenille needles, which are similar in shape to crewel needles, for coarser wools.

Frames

Some stitches are inclined to pucker the fabric, others need to be worked under tension. If the work is not too large, a square or slate frame can be used. A ring frame can be used for parts of a design on a large piece of fabric. If you plan to use some heavily textured stitches, watch out for the surrounding areas and work these first if possible to avoid damaging the thick stitches. Less textured areas can be protected from being crushed by the frame by placing tissue paper between the two rings. Tighten the screw carefully and then tear away the paper from the working area.

Stitches

These are chosen to suit the design. It is not necessary to use all the stitches in any one piece of work. One stitch well used can make a most effective piece of work. If a stitch does not make the effect you want, then it is time to look for another. Give sufficient time to try out stitches; half an inch of stitchery cannot really give you enough experience. People tend to have preferences for certain stitches, but before you reject any stitch, try it on another type of fabric or with a different type of yarn.

The fabric you use will affect the size of the individual stitch. A stitch will be large in thick wool on a coarse fabric, and small in fine wool on linen. The diagrams show the average effect.

Many stitches can be used for different purposes and the simpler stitches are often the most versatile. A stitch such as stem stitch will make a line or it can be worked to fill a space. French knots can make a solid, heavily textured area or they can be lightly worked to make a semi-solid filling. You can invent ways of using each stitch or a combination of stitches to suit yourself.

Stem stitch Work from left to right. The needle enters the fabric a little way along the line to be worked and comes out again halfway back to the beginning of the line. The next stitch goes ahead again and the needle comes out at the end of the first stitch. This makes a continuous line of back stitches on the wrong side of the fabric. To make a thicker line, let the needle take slantwise stitches.

Shapes may be filled in with stem stitch by working further rows touching each other. Do not pull too tightly.

Areas may be shaded by working the first row or rows in a light colour and then changing to progressively darker tones of the colour, or vice versa.

Stem stitch

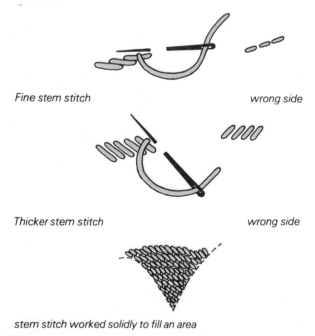

Fine stem stitch   *wrong side*

Thicker stem stitch   *wrong side*

stem stitch worked solidly to fill an area

Chain stitch Work from top to bottom. The yarn is held by the left thumb while the needle is re-inserted almost in the same hole and brought out again a little further down the line of working. The needle catches down the wool in a loop. The last stitch is held down by a tiny stitch to secure the final loop.

This can also be worked as a solid filling and shaded. It is another stitch which will pucker if pulled tightly.

Open Chain stitch This makes a broader, open line and is worked in a similar way to chain stitch except that the needle enters the fabric to the right and comes out again under the first stitch so that a ladder is made. It takes a little practice to find out how tight to pull the yarn before the stitch is completed. The angle of the needle may be varied to open or close up the 'ladder'.

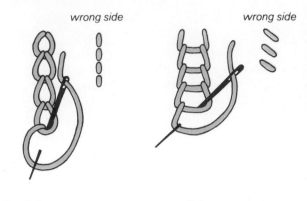

Chain stitch   *Open chain stitch*

Detached Chain This stitch is made like the last stitch in a row of chain stitch. The loop is caught down by a small stitch. The stitches can be worked at regular intervals or close together to make a semi-solid texture. If the catching down stitch is longer, the stitch has a tail which can be very attractive.

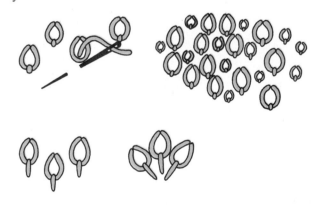

Detached chain

French Knots These give texture and need practice to work well. The yarn is scooped round the needle which is then inserted a little way behind the point where it came out. Control the loop of yarn by light pressure of the thumb nail until the length of yarn is pulled through the fabric. If the yarn is allowed to escape, the stitch usually looks untidy. As it is not easy to unpick French knots, it is best to practice first and work slowly. A larger knot can be made by twisting the yarn twice round the needle. Three or more twists are very difficult to manage and it is better to use a thicker yarn for a larger knot.

French knots

Seeding

a) Bring needle up, wrap thread round end
b) Twist needle, re-insert behind entry point
c) Bring out for next stitch, control thread with
   thumb
d) A group of knots

Long and Short stitch This takes its name from the first row of stitches to be worked which are alternately long and short. Subsequent rows are all the same length. It needs practice to arrange the stitches well within the shape. On following

Seeding This makes a similar effect to French knots, but is more delicate and flatter in texture. Each stitch is a back stitch, or two back stitches worked over each other. Following stitches are worked at an angle to the last. An area may be shaded by working the stitches closer in one part and gradually spacing them out to fade into plain fabric.

Long and short stitch (first row).
Subsequent rows are all the same length

Bellflower design sewn in satin stitch, chain stitch, detached chain, button stitch and seeding using Anchor Tapisserie Wool and Crewel.

rows bring the needle up on the end of the short stitch, working only into these alternate spaces. This enables you to judge the best angle for the new stitch. Shading is effective.

Satin stitch This is a smooth stitch which can be used for small petals, leaves and similar shapes and also for thick stems. It is usually best to work the stitches so that they are at an angle to the shape to be filled. They should never be so long that they will not lie smoothly.

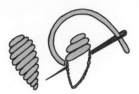

Satin stitch worked over an outline of split stitch

Split stitch This makes a very fine smooth line which is useful for delicate stems as well as for a foundation for satin stitch. It is worked in a

Split stitch (two movements)

needle enters fabric

needle brought out through thread

Leaf spray design sewn in long and short stitch and stem stitch using Anchor Stranded Cotton.

Flower spray design sewn in back-stitched wheels with split stitch stems using Anchor Stranded Cotton.

similar way to stem stitch but the needle comes up through the middle of the thread, piercing it. Complex lines like tendrils can be worked with this stitch which holds curves well.

Buttonhole stitch Work from left to right with the yarn forming a loop under the needle. It can be used as an edging stitch, either with the looped edge outwards, giving a strong line, or with the other edge outwards when it will be less dominant or of different patterns.

Semi-solid or solid fillings can be worked in buttonhole stitch and shading is possible by working the rows in lighter or darker tones.

Buttonhole stitch

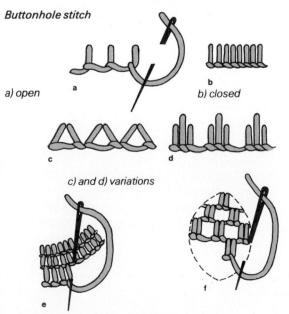

a) open

b) closed

c) and d) variations

e) and f) used as a filling worked into tops of previous row

Couched fillings These are semi-solid fillings which can be invented or copied. A grid of lines is laid over a shape and to keep the tension right a frame is essential. The grid may be made in a square or a diamond. These long stitches must be caught down. The catching stitch can be tiny and unobtrusive, or large like a cross stitch making part of the pattern. The basic grid may be left as it is or further stitches can be added. Another alternative is to make the grid of pairs of lines or even more, catching down the last stitch only, making a kind of plaid.

These stitches need fairly large areas to show off the patterns. Similar fillings can be made with stitches like buttonhole.

Couched fillings

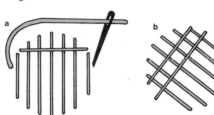

a) Laying foundation
b) Alternative diamond foundation

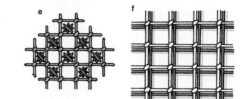

c) Securing foundation with small stitches
d) Securing foundation with large stitches

e) Double cross stitches in spaces
f) Battlemented filling

g) Close-up of f)

Wheels Wheels of various kinds (see page 15) are often incorporated in crewel work.

Pattern within pattern In traditional crewel work, large spaces were often filled in with further decoration. A big leaf might be filled in with a spray of smaller leaves, for example. This is a chance to enjoy stitching freely.

Flower head design sewn in laid fillings with French knots using Anchor Tapisserie Wool and Crewel.

CROSS STITCH

Cross stitch is a form of embroidery that can be found almost all over the world. It can be used in many different ways. European peasant embroidery, very often done in a restricted colour scheme, black and red for example, has a variety of bold designs. Victorian samples include lettering, flowers, birds, houses and even people on very fine material. Modern Danish cross stitch is designed from pressed flowers and naturalistic birds and has a delicate look.

Fabrics

You will need to use evenweave fabrics for cross stitch. These are woven with the same weight of thread in either direction and the spaces between the warp and weft are square. In some of these fabrics, the threads are grouped so that the spaces between are clearly visible. These are suitable for bold, quick work and are very useful for anyone with sight problems.

The single weave fabrics come in a variety of weights, described by the number of threads to the centimetre or inch. 18 threads to the inch will be fairly coarse and 28 or 30 threads per inch will be fine. These fabrics can be bought at specialist embroidery shops and are usually made of linen or cotton. They are fairly expensive. Sometimes it is possible to buy evenweave fabric in dress or furnishing fabric departments, but it is difficult to

Cross stitch worked as a peasant border using Anchor Pearl Cott

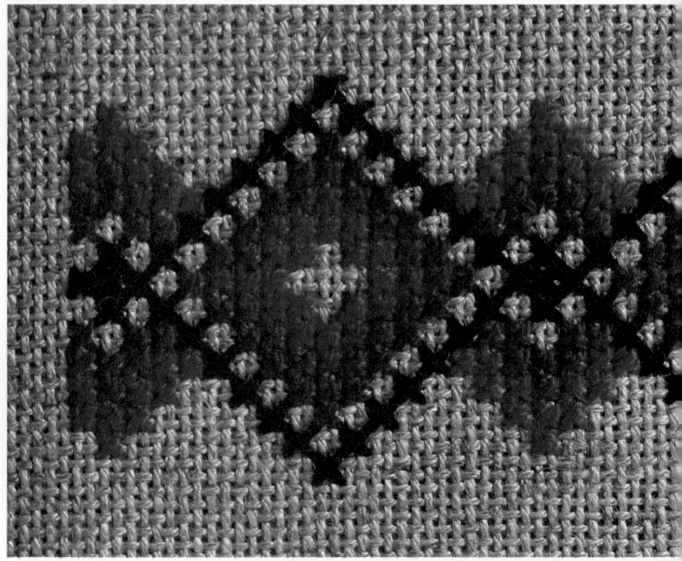

tell at sight whether any fabric is truly even-weave. If the warp is a little different in thickness from the weft, the cross stitch will be oblong, not square. This may not matter if the design is a border used one way of the fabric only — on a curtain for example, but a symmetrical design based on the form of a cross to be used on a cushion will be larger one way than the other, and no longer square.

There are some less expensive fabrics which can be used for cross stitch. Hessian is one. It is a coarse fabric, quick to work and suitable for items such as tote bags. Some of the wool canvases sold in good haberdashery departments for interlining in tailoring are evenweave or nearly so.

Threads

A single thread makes the best effect. Specialist embroidery shops sell soft embroidery cotton and Pearl cotton. There is more choice in thickness of threads and in the colour range in some makes

than others. If you cannot buy these threads easily, stranded cotton may be used. On coarse fabrics, it is also possible to use soft cotton or crochet cotton. The thickness of the thread must be chosen to suit the weight of the fabric, a coarser thread on a coarser fabric and vice versa. The cross stitch should be bold, but should not crowd its neighbour, so try out threads first on spare fabric.

Colour

Some of the most effective work is done on natural or white fabric. Many cross stitch designs loose their effect if too many colours of thread are used. This is especially true on coarse fabrics. The geometric designs are usually best if worked in one or two strong colours. It is also effective to work in white, cream or natural on dark brown, navy or black fabric. Work based on modern Danish designs uses more colours but as it is usually done on fine fabric, the colours blend very well.

Designs

There are many books on cross stitch containing charted designs. These charts show the position of every stitch. The stitch can be worked over two or more threads. A design done from a chart over two threads will work out at half the size of the same design worked over four threads. You can work out the finished size of a design by arithmetic. How many stitches to the inch or centimetre are there on the fabric and how many on the chart? A small part of the design can be worked and compared with the size on the chart.

If the design is to be worked as a border, start in the centre and work outwards towards the edges. A large square or circular design should be started in the centre of the fabric. It is a help to mark the centre of the fabric by a tacking line in each direction to act as a guide, especially where only a half or quarter of the design is charted. If you are working a border round a cloth or cushion, you must think well about turning the corner. If the size is not fixed, you can turn the corner in a good place and work it continuously. To find the best place, hold a handbag mirror diagonally across the design and move it along until you find the most pleasing effect. If the size is fixed, you may not be able to plan the corner in this way and a different motif can occupy each corner before continuing with your border.

Allow sufficient material between the border or motif and the edge. If a hem has to be made, a

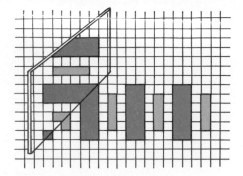

Planning a corner with a mirror held at 45°

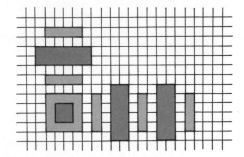

Planning a corner with a different motif

little border may be worked and the hem turned on the wrong side and slip-stitched to the cross stitches so that it cannot be seen on the right side.

Needles

Tapestry needles have long eyes and blunt points so the thread passes cleanly through the fabric without piercing the warp or weft. A packet of assorted sizes will take most threads. For very coarse threads, specialist shops sell large blunt-ended needles.

Starting and Finishing

The stitches must be secure but the fastening on and off must not show on the right side. Take the needle in about an inch and a half from where you want to begin. Tie a knot on the end of the thread. When you have worked sufficient stitches, the knot is cut off and the end threaded into the back of the work, with a small back stitch to stop it pulling out. You may find it easier to do this with a crewel or a chenille needle, both of which have points. Fasten off into the back of the work with a few small stitches.

Cross Stitch

Stitches must be crossed in the same direction all over the work to get the best effect. The usual way is to work the stitch as shown in the diagram, but if you are left-handed you may find it easier to work the reverse way.

Cross stitch (method 1).

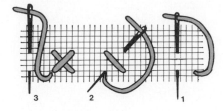

Completing each cross in turn

There are two ways of working. Each stitch can be completed before beginning the next, or if there are several stitches in a row, half of the stitch is worked in one direction and completed on the return journey. This can be done in vertical or horizontal rows, according to the design, but keep to the same direction in any one area. Practice to get the tension right. The embroidery thread should not distort the fabric, nor should it appear slack. If the stitch looks loose, you may be working over too many threads, or with too fine a thread.

Cross stitch (method 2)

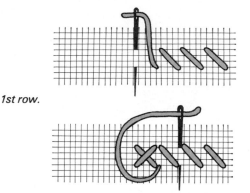

1st row.

Return journey.

Long-armed Cross stitch Each cross is completed in turn, as shown. The first half of the stitch going forward passes over twice as many threads as the second half going backward.

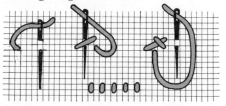

Long armed cross stitch (also showing stitches on back of work)

Traditional Assisi work using Anchor Pearl Cotton.

Assisi work Named after Assisi in Italy, the design is outlined with double running stitch, usually in black, and the background is worked in cross stitch, or one of the variations of cross stitch, in a strong colour, blue or red, for example. Tradi-

Assisi work:

outlines partly worked in double running stitch

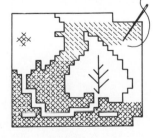

Cross stitch background being worked.

tionally, Assisi work is done on loosely-woven linen or cotton, the motifs being outlined in black and the background filled with china blue.

Method Start by outlining the motifs in double running stitch in a dark colour. The needle makes two journeys as described. The cross stitch background should also be worked in two journeys and make sure that all the top threads of the crosses lie in the same direction.

Double Running stitch This stitch (also known as Holbein stitch) should be worked over the same number of threads as the cross stitch. As its name suggests, it is basically a simple running stitch. On one journey the needle goes in and out of the fabric. At the end of the journey, the work is turned and the needle runs back to fill in the spaces. Notice the way that the needle slants.

Double running stitch

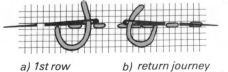

a) 1st row   *b) return journey*

PULLED FABRIC

Pulled Fabric work is a most beautiful and practical form of embroidery. With the knowledge of only a few basic stitches, a very attractive and professional looking article can be made. It is not the same as Drawn Thread work where threads are taken out (or withdrawn) from the fabric, but in this technique the threads are pulled together to create the pattern.

Pulled work has traditionally been used for household linen for many generations. It was generally worked on linen in neutral colours (white, cream, natural) with toning thread. However, evenweave fabrics are available now in a variety of colours and pleasing results in pulled fabric work can be obtained using matching or toning threads.

Fabric

Evenweave material (i.e. the same number of threads per inch or centimetre for warp and weft) must be used. The more threads there are to the inch or centimetre the finer the work will be. All the samples shown are worked on linen 21 threads to 2.5cm (1in).

Linen gives the best results but there are many man-made fibres from which a very satisfactory article can be made. The latter have the advantage of being cheaper and more easily laundered, which is especially to be recommended for something which will be frequently in the wash. The beginner should beware of any material which is too loosely woven as the end result could be extremely disappointing.

Below: A sample of Honeycomb stitch; below right: a sample of Wave stitch using Anchor Pearl Cotton.

Threads

The most suitable threads are Pearl cotton, soft embroidery cotton and crochet cotton. Stranded cotton can be used but this does tend to wear or go fuzzy with the constant pulling. The samples shown are worked in Anchor Pearl Cotton No 8 for the pulled stitches and Anchor Pearl Cotton No 5 for the satin stitch.

Needles

Tapestry, i.e. blunt needles, should be used as pointed or sharp needles will split the threads of the fabric. No 24 is a good size for most work.

Starting

Before starting the work all edges must be oversewn to prevent the material from fraying. An embroidery frame can be used but this is purely a

matter of choice.

To begin the stitching, darn the thread in neatly on the back of the work. Finish off with a small back stitch in a part which will eventually be covered by the embroidery.

All stitches, with the exception of satin stitch, must be firmly pulled to create the holes. It is the holes, rather than the stitches themselves which create the pattern.

Design

The most common design for this type of embroidery is geometrical, as the regularity of the stitches lend themselves particularly well to squares, rectangles, etc. Experience gives confidence and one can then design more freely. Simple forms such as buildings, birds, animals, flowers and trees adapt easily to pulled work, a variety of stitches being used for the shape, and satin stitch or a couched thread for the outline.

Designs should first be drawn on graph paper, each line representing one thread of the fabric. The size of the design will, of course, depend on the number of threads in the fabric.

Before starting the embroidery, run a tacking thread in a contrasting colour across both the length and width of the material. These will serve as a guide when working the design.

A geometric design can be worked straight on to the fabric. If it is to be a border, then work the first line from the centre out to the edge otherwise the design could be lopsided. If only a corner is to be embroidered, then it can be started a certain number of threads from the edge — your eye will be the best judge as to how far this is.

All the stitches can be varied in size by stitching over more, or less, threads than the numbers stated. The fewer the number of threads, the smaller the stitch will be.

Stitches

The stitches for Pulled Fabric are pulled tightly, producing a pattern of holes. In this way they are unlike many embroidery stitches which lie on the surface. The following are some basic stitches. Two are worked vertically, two are worked horizontally and two are worked diagonally.

Honeycomb stitch This is worked from the top downwards. Bring the thread out at the arrow and insert it two (or however many you wish)

threads to the right at A, bring it out two threads down at B, insert it again at A and bring it out again at B. Insert it two threads to the left at C and bring it out two threads down at D. Insert it again at C and bring it out again at D. Continue like this for the required length then turn the work round and work the next row in exactly the same way. The second diagram shows the start of the second row, the third shows two rows completed.

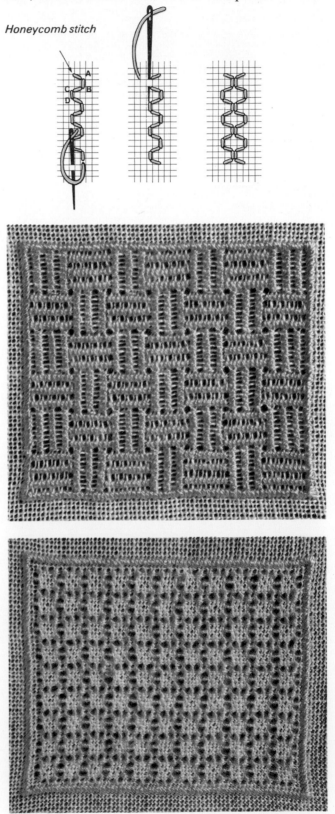

Honeycomb stitch

Above right: A sample of Chessboard filling; below right: a sample of Ringed Back stitch (instructions overleaf) using Anchor Pearl Cotton.

Chessboard Filling stitch This is another stitch which is worked vertically, i.e. from the top to the bottom. It consists of blocks of satin stitch each over three threads and each block is made up of three rows of ten stitches. The blocks alternate horizontally and vertically. (This is the one exception where satin stitch is pulled tightly). The diagram shows the layout of the stitches, beginning at the arrow.

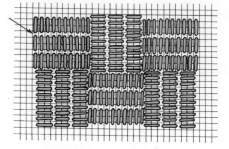

Chessboard filling stitch

Diagonal raised band using Anchor Pearl Cotton.

Wave stitch This stitch is worked alternately from right to left and from left to right. The diagram shows the method of working. Bring the needle out at A and insert it at B, four threads down and two threads to the right. Bring it out at C four threads to the left and then insert it at A. Bring it out at D, four threads to the left and insert it at C, four threads down and two to the right. Now bring it out at E, four threads to the left. Continue like this to the end of the row at H in diagram 2 and then insert the needle at F and bring it out at G, i.e. eight threads down. Turn the work upside down, and work back again in the same way.

it out two threads down and four to the left at C, again insert it at A and bring it out again at C and insert it once more at A. Next bring it out at D, two threads up and four to the left, insert it at C, bring it out again at D and insert it again at C. Continue like this to the end of the row. Turn the work upside down and repeat the first row taking care to see that the second row starts at the arrow on row 2. As the work progresses it will be seen that there are *four* stitches on *each* of the vertical and horizontal stitches.

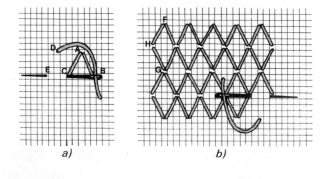

a)   b)

Wave stitch

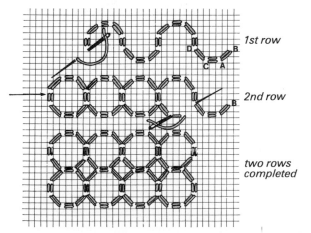

Ringed back stitch

Ringed Back stitch This is another horizontal stitch and is most effective. It does, however, require a little more concentration to master it, but the result is well worth the effort. The rings will not be seen until the second row has been worked. First row, bring the needle out at A then insert it two threads up and two to the right at B. Bring it out at A and insert it again at B. Next bring

Faggot stitch This stitch is worked diagonally, starting at the top right-hand corner of the work. It is also known as diagonal square stitch but the square (as in the case of ringed back stitch) will not be seen until the second row has been completed. The method of working is shown in the diagram. Bring the needle out at A and insert it

A pin stitch hem using Anchor Pearl Cotton.

threads down and three to the left. Continue in this way to the end of the row. For the second row, bring the needle out three threads down and three to the left of the *last* upright stitch at E. Insert it six threads to the right at F. (It will be seen that this is the same hole as the top of the second upright stitch of the previous row). Next bring the needle out three threads down and three to the left at G. Continue in this way to the end of the row. The stitch should be pulled very tight to produce the ridged effect.

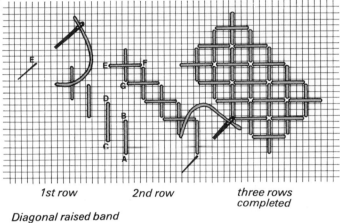

| 1st row | 2nd row | three rows completed |

Diagonal raised band

four threads to the right at B. Next bring it out four threads down and four to the left at C (i.e. four threads below A). Insert it at A and bring it out again four threads down and four to the left at D, insert it again at C. Continue like this to the end of the row and then turn work upside down and work back in the same way.

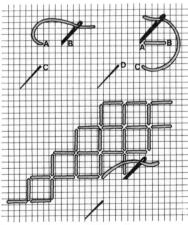

Faggot stitch

Diagonal raised band This stitch has more texture than those given previously. It produces diagonal ridges as its name suggests. The method of working is shown in the diagram. The stitch is, in effect, an upright cross stitch, and again is not completed until the end of the second row. The vertical part of the stitch is worked on the first row and the horizontal part on the second row. Bring the needle out at A in the bottom right-hand corner and insert it six threads up at B, bring it out three threads down and three to the left at C. Insert it six threads up at D and bring it out three

A Pin stitch hem The plain edge shown is a pin stitch hem. First tack the hem on the wrong side — taking care to tack straight along one thread and also to mitre the corners (see below).

For the pin stitch bring the thread out at the arrow in diagram 1, insert it two threads down at A. Bring it out the required number of threads to the left at B (in this case four threads). Insert it at A again and then bring it out once more at B. Insert it again at A and then bring it out two threads up at C (diagram 2) taking care to stitch through the extra thickness of the hem.

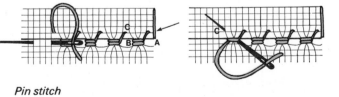

Pin stitch

Mitred Corner To mitre a corner, fold and press the hem, open it out and fold the corner across on the inner fold. Cut off the corner (leaving just enough for a small seam). Refold the hem and slipstitch along the diagonal line.

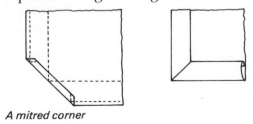

A mitred corner

SMOCKING

Smocking is a decorative way of controlling fullness in fabric. The gathering is done with spaced rows of tacking (basting) worked from the back, which are drawn up to the required width. Rows of stitches are then worked in embroidery thread on the front. When the work is complete, the gathering threads are withdrawn.

Smocking can be used on all sorts of garments where fullness is required such as blouses, skirts, aprons, dresses, lingerie and children's clothes. It can also be used in the home to make such things as cushions, lampshades, fixed curtains, tablecloths and pelmets and many other useful and decorative items.

Fabrics

Most fabrics, plain or printed, natural or man-made, which will drape suitably for the purpose can be used. Very thick or heavy fabrics are not recommended for beginners. Striped, checked and spotted fabrics are especially suitable for smocking as the pattern can be used as a guide for the gathering threads.

As a general rule, three times the finished width of the smocked area is required. This varies somewhat with the fabric, the distance between gathers, the stitch and the tension.

Threads

Use a strong cotton or cotton/polyester sewing thread for the gathers, in a contrasting colour. Embroidery threads such as stranded cotton, soft embroidery cotton and Perle cotton, are used for the stitchery on the front of the work.

Needles

Crewel embroidery needles are most useful as they have a sharp point and a long eye.

Preparation of Fabric

All preparation is done on the wrong side of the fabric. Always press the fabric to begin with, and oversew the edges if they are likely to fray.

Seam pieces of fabric together first if they are to be smocked in one continuous piece.

If you have not done any smocking before, work a small sample before beginning the project. This will give you some idea of the tension and the appearance of the stitchery.

Marking the Fabric for Gathering

The fabric has to be gathered evenly. This can be achieved in several ways: by ironing a smocking dot transfer on the back; by using a gauge, by counting the threads or by picking up marks on a regular pattern.

Smocking dot transfers These are used on the wrong side of the fabric. They are available at embroidery and haberdashery shops. The spacing between the dots varies. Generally the closer the dots and rows, the finer the fabric used. The

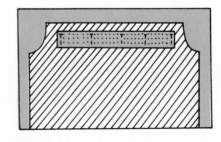

Smocking dot transfer

most usual size has 5mm between the dots. The maker's name which is printed on the edge of the transfer must be cut off. This is used for testing on the wrong side of a scrap of fabric. The iron

Transfer pinned in position, wax side down on wrong side of fabric

should be at the right temperature to transfer the dots quickly. Extra care is essential when ironing on to man-made fabrics. Sometimes the dots come through to the right side. These will wash

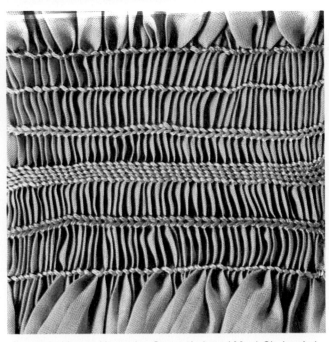

A sample of smocking using Stem stitch and Mock Chain stitch. Row 1: Stem; row 2: Stem; row 3: Mock Chain; row 4: Braid; row 5: Mock Chain; row 6: Stem using Anchor Stranded Cotton.

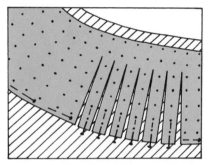

Transfer slashed to allow for curve

out. For curved smocking, as in a rounded yoke, the transfer is slashed to fit the area as shown.

When estimating the depth of smocking, allow one row extra for joining onto a yoke, etc. This becomes the seam line and gives a smooth join.

Gauge If smocking dots are not available, a guide can be made from thin card and marked on the wrong side of the fabric with a transfer pencil which washes out. Test before transferring.

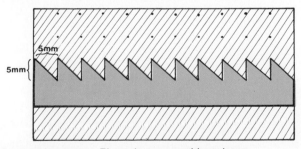

A smocking gauge. The points are positioned on a row of dots and the next row is marked at the base of each V

Counting the threads On a loosely woven fabric it is sometimes possible to count the warp and weft threads and pick up systematically.

Patterned fabrics On check, dot and stripe fabrics the pattern will form a guide for picking up the fabric at regular intervals.

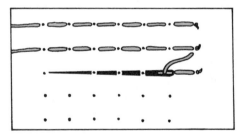

Regularly spaced gathering on striped fabric

Gathering the Fabric

Work on the wrong side as follows:
1 In a contrasting colour to the background, cut one length of thread, longer than the row of dots, for each row to be gathered.
2 Thread needle and put a large and firm knot in the end of the thread.
3 Work from right to left, picking up each dot. At the end of the row, leave the thread hanging. Work each row in the same way.

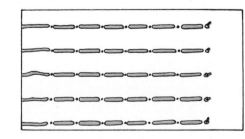

Regular gathering on wrong side, picking up each dot

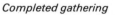

Completed gathering

Tying the threads
1 Pull up each gathering thread to the required width.
2 Tie together in pairs at the ends of rows.
3 Cut threads to within several inches.

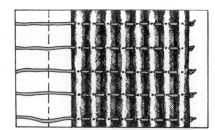

Pulling up the gathers

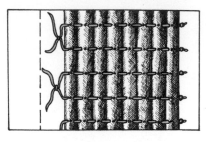

Tying the ends of threads in pairs

It is not easy to gauge how much to gather the work. There should be enough space between each fold for a needle to be inserted. By working a small sample first, in the fabric to be used, you can determine the tension that suits you.

Smocking

The embroidery is worked on the right side of the gathered panel. As a general rule, pick up approximately 1mm of each fold and try to work to an even tension throughout.

The stitches are worked with the needle parallel to the gathering threads. The first row of gathers is left for joining, i.e. onto a yoke, etc. You will find that stitches vary in elasticity, some are tight and some are loose.

Starting Start with a knot and come up from the back, coming out on the left hand side of the first fold.

Finishing End by taking the needle through to the back beside the last fold. Work two small stitches on the nearest fold at the back, so that they will not be visible from the front.

Joining If the thread for working is not long enough to complete the row, finish as above. Start off again with a knot as above making the join as inconspicuous as possible.

A sample of Double Cable and Basket stitches. Row 1: Stem; row 2: Cable; row 3: Double Cable; row 4: Basket; row 5: Double Cable; row 6: Cable using Anchor Stranded Cotton.

Stitches

Smocking stitches are very simple and are mostly based on stem stitch. Keep the needle parallel to the gathering thread, and note whether the thread should be above or below the needle. Except for Vandyke stitch, all the following stitches are worked from left to right.

Stem or Outline stitch A firm stitch which is often used for the top row of smocking. Bring needle out at the left of the first fold of the line to be worked and, keeping the thread below the needle, take a stitch over each fold in turn across the line. Keep the needle parallel to the row.

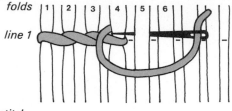

Stem stitch

Mock Chain Work one row of stem. Immediately below this work another row of stem, but this time with the thread above the needle. This is a tight stitch.

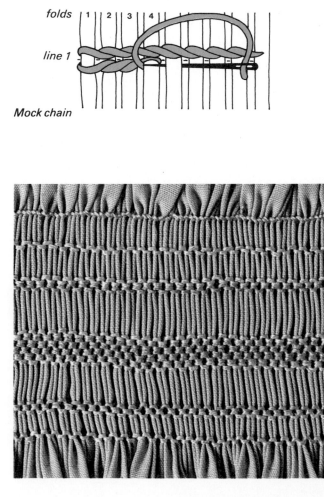

Mock chain

Cable stitch Bring the needle out to the left of the first fold on line 1. With thread below needle, take a stitch over the second fold. With thread above needle take a stitch over the third fold. Continue to end of row keeping thread alternately above and below needle.

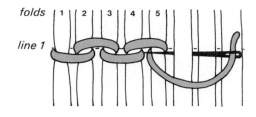

Cable stitch

Double Cable Work one row of cable, starting with thread below needle. Work another row immediately beneath the first row, starting with thread above needle.

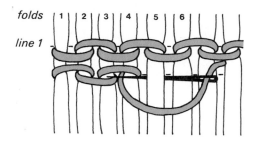

Double cable

Basket stitch Work several rows of double cable. This is a tight stitch.

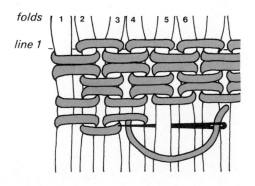

Basket stitch

Wave stitch This is basically stem stitch worked in a wave pattern. Bring the needle out on the left of the first fold on line 1. With thread below needle, take a stitch over the second fold at a

A sample of Wave and Trellis stitches. Row 1: Stem; row 2: Wave; row 3 and 4: Trellis; row 5: Wave; row 6: Close wave using Anchor Stranded Cotton.

slightly higher level, then over the fourth and fifth folds depending on the height of the 'wave'. The thread is kept below the needle on the way up and above it on the way down. Keep the needle parallel to the gathering threads. This is an elastic stitch.

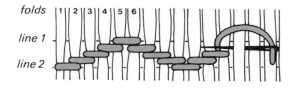

Wave stitch

Trellis stitch This consists of rows of wave stitch arranged to form a trellis pattern.

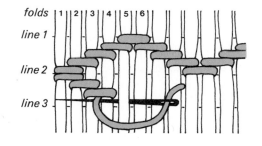

Trellis stitch

Diamond stitch Each row is worked across two lines. Bring the needle out at the first fold on line 1. With thread above needle make a stitch over the second fold. Drop down to line 2, and with thread above needle make a stitch over the third fold. With thread below needle, make a stitch over the fourth fold. Return to line 1, and with thread below needle make a stitch over the fifth fold, with thread above needle make a stitch over the sixth fold. Continue to the end of the row.

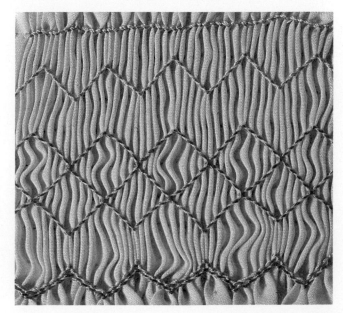

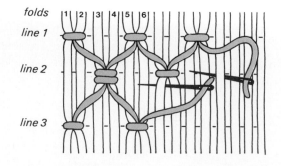

Diamond stitch

Start the next row at line 3, and work up and down to line 2, meeting the previous row as shown.

Vandyke stitch Work from right to left. Bring the needle out on the left of the second fold on line 2. With thread below the needle, take a stitch over the first two folds. Move up to line 1 and pass the needle through the second and third folds, then make a stitch over them. Move down to line 2, pass the needle through the third and fourth folds, then with thread below needle take a stitch over them.

Continue stitching from line 1 to line 2 across the row. On the next row, work between lines 3 and 2.

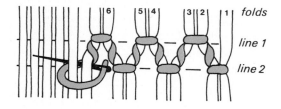

Vandyke stitch

Honeycomb Bring the needle out at the first fold on line 1. With thread above needle, make a stitch

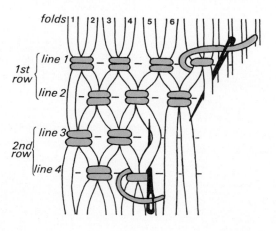

Honeycomb

over the first and second folds. Make another stitch, this time slipping the needle down the second fold to come out at line 2. With thread below needle, make a stitch over the second and third folds. Make another stitch, slipping the needle up the third fold to come out on line 1. The next row is worked on lines 3 and 4.

Surface Honeycomb Bring the needle out on the left of the first fold of line 2. With thread below needle, make a stitch over the second fold, then over the same fold again on line 1 above. With thread above needle, make a stitch over the third fold, then again over the same fold on line 2 below. Work across the row between lines 2 and 1. The next row starts in the same place as the first row and works across between lines 2 and 3.

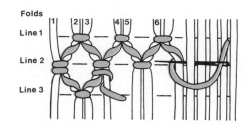

Surface honeycomb

Embroidery stitches used in smocking Folds can be held together with feather, herringbone and chain stitches. Other stitches for decoration are Bullion for rosebuds, and Lazy daisy for flowers and leaves.

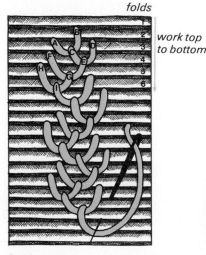

Feather stitch

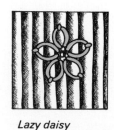

Lazy daisy

Herringbone stitch

A sample of Diamond and Stem stitches. Row 1: Stem; row 2: Diamond using Anchor Stranded Cotton and Anchor Pearl Cotton.

A sample of Vandyke and Stem stitches. Row 1: Stem; row 2: rows of Vandyke using Anchor Pearl Cotton.

Chain stitch

Bullion stitch

Finishing

When a smocked piece is finished it is pressed as follows:-

1 Place wrong side upwards.

2 Steam well with a steam iron. If this is not available, lay a damp cloth over the work and pass a hot iron lightly over, taking care not to flatten it.

3 Remove all gathering threads.

4 Neaten the edges if necessary with a very fine pin tuck on the wrong side, as close as possible to the end folds.

Stretching

Sometimes smocking is worked too tightly. In this case take out the gathering threads, lay the work wrong side up on the ironing board, and pin out to size. Steam press as above.

A sample of Surface Honeycomb. Row 1: Stem; row 2: rows of Surface Honeycomb using Anchor Stranded Cotton.

MACHINE EMBROIDERY

Beautiful effects can be achieved by machine embroidery without any great technical knowledge or skill. All the examples here are worked in straight stitch, zig-zag or automatic pattern on an electric machine with the ordinary foot or the darning foot in place.

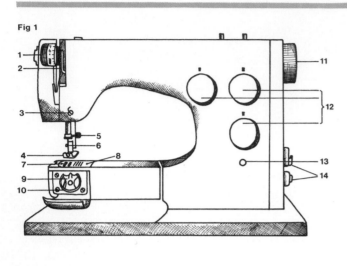

Fig 1

The sewing machine

1 Top thread tension guide
2 Thread guide
3 Thread guide
4 Presser foot
5 Needle clamp screw
6 Needle
7 Feed dog
8 Throat plate
9 Spool case
10 Plate holding spool case
11 Hand wheel
12 Knobs for stitch length, width, patterns etc.
13 Drop feed control
14 Spool threading mechanism

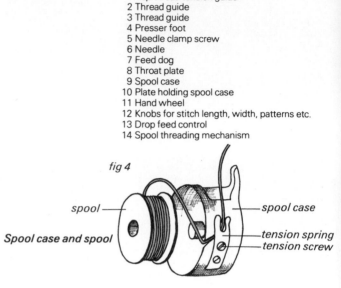

fig 4

spool — spool case
Spool case and spool — tension spring — tension screw

Requirements

Ideally, a machine used for embroidery should have:-

1 A swing needle.
2 A spool case that can be removed each time the spool is filled, not just the spool itself.
3 The ability to use a twin needle.
4 A reverse feed, preferably with a press button.
5 The facility to lower the teeth and use a darning foot.

All these requirements can be found on a reasonably priced machine. A straight stitch machine should be electric, as both hands are needed to control the work.

Needles

Machine needles come in two kinds, those for the expensive precision machines, and those for the ordinary machines. The precision needles are marked 705H. They have a curved cutout at the back of the needle near the point, which allows for extreme accuracy in directing the needle. The non-precision needles are marked 130. Any pack marked 130/705H will do for all machines.

High numbers indicate thicker needles. The instruction manual will supply a table of suggested needles for different fabrics, but this does not always apply for machine embroidery.

You will find it better to use a large needle (100/18) even for fine fabrics, as it is strong and will not bend when using different threads. Always use ball point needles for knitted fabrics.

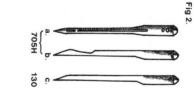

Needles

Twin needles Twin needles are used for a double row of stitching, and two-colour effects. Straight stitch can produce an effect very like corded quilting. Check that your make of machine will take a twin needle. You would only use a twin needle with an ordinary foot on the machine.

There are two types of twin needle:
Version A usually fixes into the normal (central) position, and has a narrow space between the needles. This version must be used for all zig-zag or automatic patterns, as there is a limited space (the slot where the needles go down) for the total stitch.

Twin needles

Version B has a wide space between the needles and is only used for straight stitch. If it is fixed to one side, the needle position must be moved before the needles will descend centrally.

Tensions

There are two tensions making up a stitch, one for the top thread and one for the bottom.

The top tension is usually controlled by a dial above the needle or on top of the machine. The top thread goes through it between two discs which press together against the thread. Sometimes the dial will be numbered from 0–8, and the larger the number the tighter the tensions will be. Otherwise the dial may show plus and minus signs, which signify tighter and looser tensions.

The bottom tension is controlled by a flat sprung piece of metal screwed to the side of the spool case. This can be held by one or two screws. If there are two, then the larger one is the one to alter for the tension. The piece of metal goes across the slit down which the thread slides, and the tighter you turn the screw the more the metal presses on the thread and tightens the tension. Only move the screw a fraction at a time as it is very sensitive.

For normal work the top and bottom tensions should be equal. If different colours are used top and bottom you will be able to see if the stitch interlocks within the thickness of the fabric. If one thread remains flat on the fabric, pulling through little loops of the other thread, then the flat one is too tight. Loosen this tight tension so that the stitch evens up.

fig 5

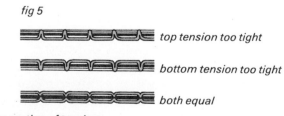

top tension too tight

bottom tension too tight

both equal

Cross-section of tensions

Right: Patterns using a narrow twin needle. a) Straight lines b) Zig-zag c) Curves d) Automatic pattern, two colours on top e) Turning corners f) Wrong side g) Straight patterns h) Tighter tension raises a ridge i) Quilting with one layer of wadding, using wide and narrow needles.

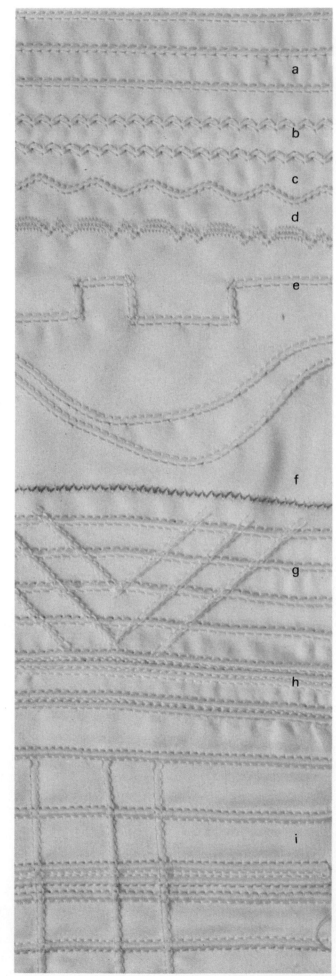

a

b

c

d

e

f

g

h

i

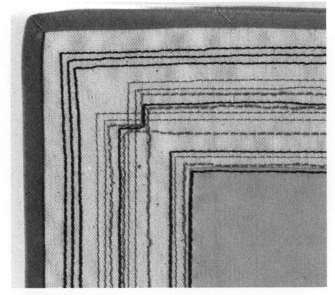

A sample showing how to link fabrics with a straight stitch pattern.

Always try the stitch out on the fabric you will use and *with the same number of layers*. If you then change the stitch to a zig zag the tension will *look* tighter, but will work well. If you require a satin stitch then you will have to loosen the top tension so that the threads lie evenly on the surface.

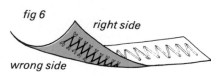

fig 6

right side

wrong side

Tension for satin

Threads

The threads used will vary according to the type of stitch and fabric. Always try out stitches on the same number of layers that will be used. Fine sewing cotton is a good all-round thread for decorative purposes, even on man-made fabrics. It is strong, satinised, and easy to tension. Use a 100 needle with it for most fabrics. For a bolder look use buttonhole twist or topstitching thread as the top thread with fine sewing cotton underneath, and loosen the top tension by approximately one number to take the thicker thread.

If you use a thicker thread on top, go as slowly and evenly as possible.

Any thread too thick to go in a 100 needle will have to be wound on the spool, and in this case the fabric will have to be worked wrong way up.

Using Thicker Spool Threads

Use smooth threads, not irregular or hairy ones. Crepe knitting wool is suitable, also thicker em-

broidery or crochet threads, perle cotton 3 or 5, soft embroidery cotton and stranded cotton. All these will have to be wound on to the spool by hand. Put the spool on the machine, hold the thread yourself, and use the motor to fill the spool as usual.

It is advisable to buy a second spool case to use for thicker threads, as the tension will have to be altered. The first one can be kept unaltered for dressmaking and ordinary sewing.

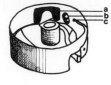

Spoolcase

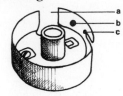

Spoolcase without spring
a) Gap, or large hole
b) Medium hole
c) Normal hole under spring

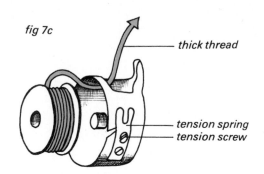

fig 7c

thick thread

tension spring
tension screw

Spool loaded with thicker thread

Threading the spool case Hold the case in the normal filling position, and pass the end of the spool thread up through the gap after the end of the tension spring, thus avoiding tension. Drop in the spool and check that the thread flows through easily. Place case in the machine. Use fine sewing cotton on top with normal tension. The thick thread will stay underneath, therefore you must stitch your fabric wrong side up. Start gently holding both threads down. Try a large straight stitch at first, then a wide open zig zag. All threads vary according to their texture and only experimenting will achieve the required effect. If the threads come out too loopy, try removing the tension spring of the spool case altogether and put the thread through the normal slit and out through the small hole at the end. This restricts the thread somewhat, thus preventing it from looping. Once the tension spring is removed you can put your thread through any hole on the side of the spool case. The further away the hole is from the end of the spring, the tighter the stitch appears to come.

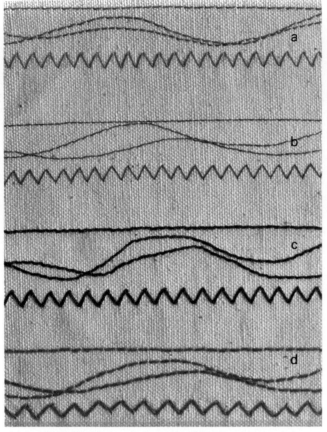

Above: Straight stitch and zig-zag in different threads. a) Fine sewing thread b) Machine thread c) Button thread d) Pearl cotton.

Transferring Designs

If working on the wrong side of the fabric, the design can be drawn out with a soft sharp pencil. On the right side, you can either work through tracing paper marked with the design, or tack out the design in the same colour of thread that will be used for the embroidery, in case you cannot un-pick it.

Hints Before Starting Work

Nearly all machine embroidery pulls up the fabric slightly so allow plenty of room round the working area. In making garments, any tucks must be stitched before the paper pattern is initially laid over the fabric.

Right: Working from the back with thick thread in the spool through small or next hole, no tension spring. a) Anchor Soft Embroidery Cotton (top row: darning foot; bottom row: ordinary foot) b) Crêpe knitting wool (top row: darning foot; bottom row: ordinary foot) c) Knitting wool (top row: darning foot; bottom row: ordinary foot) d) Coats Chain Mercer Crochet Cotton (ordinary foot) e) Anchor Pearl Cotton (top row: darning foot; bottom row: ordinary foot) f) Lurex crochet thread (top row: ordinary foot; bottom row: darning foot).

52

If the fabric is thin or loosely woven, back it with tissue paper and work through the paper, which can be torn away when the stitching is complete.

Always try and hold the fabric with both hands as much as possible, keeping it taut across the straight grain. This helps to prevent puckering.

A Gentle Start

Consult the handbook for instructions on threading up the machine. Make sure both upper and lower threads lead out towards the back, and lay your finger on them to keep them in place while you turn the drive wheel gently with the other hand. Let the motor take over very gradually. If you always make a careful start like this you will have no trouble with threads jamming or needle unthreading.

Straight stitch Straight stitchery with the foot in place can be made very decorative when the thickness and colour of the thread and the spacing of the lines is varied. Straight stitch can be used for Applique, Quilting, Patchwork (see separate chapters).

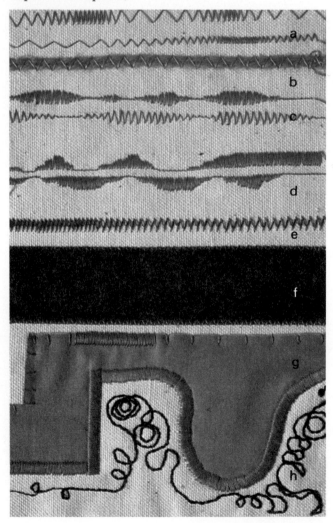

Try the reverse feed while you are stitching. If the fabric is guided slightly sideways it will produce angular pointed lines.

Ribbon and lace can be applied with a straight stitch, and should be tacked or pinned well before being sewn down. All ribbon and lace should be washed before being applied.

Zig Zag stitch The larger the number on the stitch length dial (or lever) the wider apart the stitches become. If a long length of stitch is used, then the zig zag is very open. As the length is reduced the stitch closes up until it becomes satin stitch.

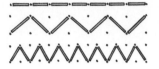

The length of the stitch operates the closeness of the zig-zag

Wrong side The uneven tension of the wrong side of a satin stitch zig zag can be used on the right side, especially if two colours are used. Altering the width emphasises the texture.

Altering the width The width can be altered as you work. Try straight lines first, then a curve. You will not cause any damage if the machine is going, it is only when the machine is stationary and the needle in the fabric that the width should not be altered. If the needle position is in the centre it will alter equally on both sides. If the needle position is left or right it will remain straight on that side and vary on the other side.

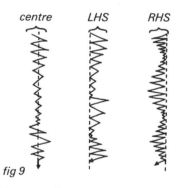

Altering widths with different needle positions.

Uses of Zig-zag and free machining. a) Zig-zag, altering length of stitch b) Thick thread couched with Zig-zag c) Satin stitch altering width d) Satin stitch as above with needle to one side e) Wrong side, showing tighter tension f) Ribbon applied with small open Zig-zag g) Applied shape, showing tacking, position of Zig-zag stitch on edge of shape, a corner and a curve h) Free machining with the darning foot, using buttonhole thread.

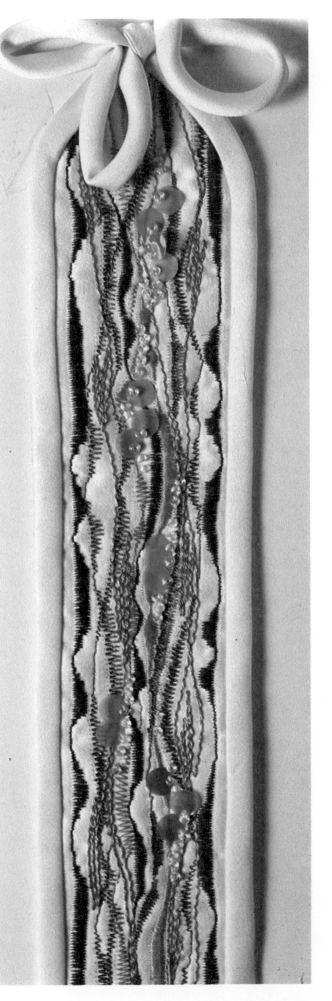

Corners Try to avoid overlapping on corners as this causes the stitching to pile up. The following method is better:

1 Work to the corner, stop with the needle on the inside of the shape (left hand side) in the fabric.

2 Lift the foot, turn the corner, put the foot down again — it is now off the shape. Use the drive wheel by hand to move the needle away from the fabric.

3 Lift the presser foot and slide the shape back into line with the needle.

4 Lower the foot and continue stitching to the next corner.

To turn a curve keep stopping with the needle on the outside of the curve in the fabric, lift the foot, shift fabric slightly, lower foot and continue. This may need to be done every few stitches if it is a really small curve. The width of stitch overlaps itself round the curve leaving no gaps.

Points Put the needle position to the right and narrow the zig zag as you approach the point, starting where the wider zig zag would have overlapped. Leave a very small width at the point. Re-position the fabric when you turn round to come back. The straight edge will stay on the outside of the shape.

Turning a corner with a twin needle You can turn a corner so that each corner matches and no stitches are missing. Operating the drive wheel by hand, bring the needles down poised above the fabric for the next stitch. Lift the foot, turn the corner putting the outside needle back in its outside position in the fabric. Lower the foot and continue stitching. The inside thread forms a triangle across the corner.

Zig-zag turning a corner

work towards corner

stop on inside

turn corner, turn wheel, poise needle

lift foot, bring fabric back into line, continue

completed corner

Combining stitches using a combination of Straight stitch, Satin stitch, Zig-zag and automatic patterns, with added beads and sequins.

RH needle position

start tapering off

turn, reposition needle; work on other side

Zig-zag. Working a point

Couching thick thread To apply a thick thread, set the machine to a wide open zig zag. Use fine sewing cotton top and bottom, and use the presser or cording foot. Position the wool under the foot and bring it up through the slit, so that it lies on the stitching line. Lower the foot and machine as usual, guiding the wool without pulling it.

Couching thick thread

Ribbons Velvet is best applied with a narrow open zig-zag going off the edge of the ribbon. Tack with a tiny stab stitch. If a straight ribbon follows a curved hemline, tack and stitch the outer curve first. Easing the inner curve to fit, pin, tack and stitch this last. A straight stitch on ribbon tends to wrinkle it across. Wash all but nylon ribbon before applying it to fabric.

Machined circles using Zig-zag, Satin stitch, Couching and Hem stitching with added beads and sequins.

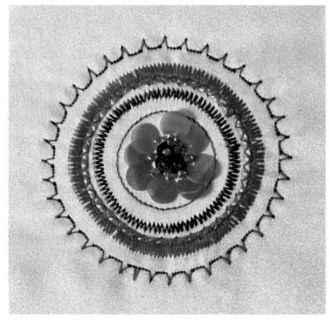

Satin stitch Satin stitch is worked by zig-zagging with the smallest possible length of stitch. To give a smooth look to the top thread, loosen the top tension by one number. The spool thread should stay underneath and will appear tighter, but do not actually tighten the spool thread or the fabric will pucker. Use tissue paper underneath soft thin fabrics. A good satin stitch makes a very decorative line, and is useful for lace, ribbon or simple applique. On striped fabric satin stitches can be used to change the stripes. Satin stitch makes a good top stitch over seams, and a neat finish to binding or piping.

Automatic patterns These vary with every machine. Having practised them with ordinary cotton and the usual tension, try using different colours and thicknesses of thread, and try the effect of combining them with ordinary zig zag, blind hemming stitch, couching, or even a straight stitch in an unusual thread.

Machining a Circle

Set the machine to the required zig-zag or automatic pattern. Place a drawing pin upside down on the machine arm, to the left of the presser foot, in line with the needle, and tape it down. Mark the centre of the required circle on the fabric with a pencil dot, and press the fabric on to the drawing pin at the marked point. Smooth out the fabric under the presser foot. Lower the foot and run the machine gently, letting the fabric turn a full circle.

Machined circles

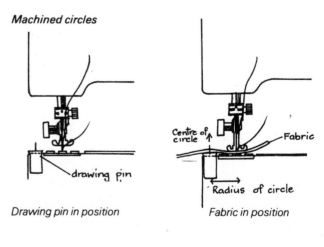

Drawing pin in position

Fabric in position

The Darning Foot

This has a sprung mechanism in it, allowing it to rise and fall with the needle so that you can move the fabric freely while you work. The teeth are lowered or covered with a separate plate. You can produce free form shapes and interesting textures, and move in any direction. The darning

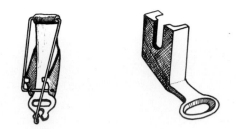

Two types of darning foot

Always start with the needle lowered, and holding the thread ends down with the left hand. Start the machine and then use both hands to guide the fabric. Use an even speed and move the fabric steadily. Smoothness is of the essence. Remember that the speed with which you move the fabric now determines the length of stitch (because you have lowered the teeth).

foot can be used either with the needle threaded normally — working right side up — or with thicker threads in the spool working with the wrong side up.

Quilting by machine using one layer of wadding.
a) Automatic pattern b) Twin needle c) Applied lace
d) Satin stitch.

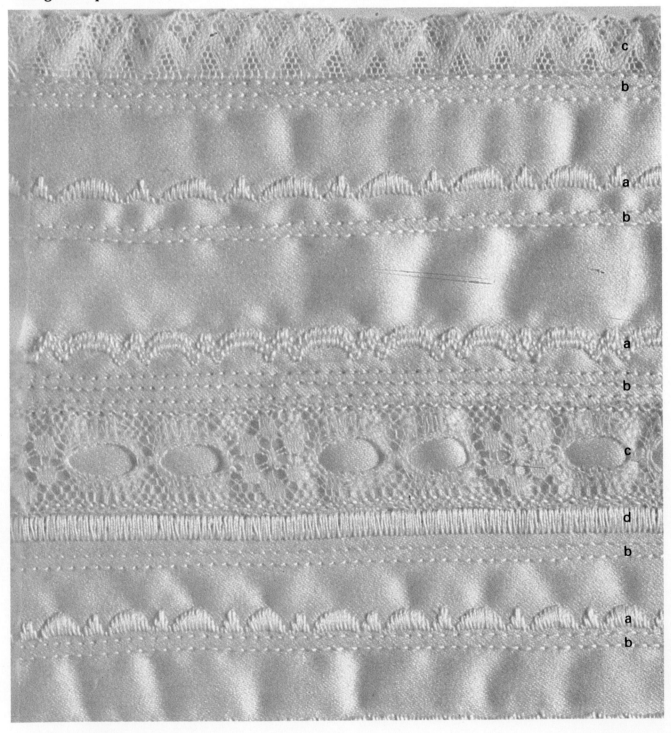

Fabric Craft

PATCHWORK

Patchwork consists of stitching together, by various means, pieces of fabric of different colours, shapes and sizes to make an attractive whole. It was one of the old thrift crafts in the days when it was necessary to use up every scrap or fabric. Today it is still useful as a money saver, but whether you are keen to use up scraps of whether you wish to create specific patterns and colour schemes, it is a stimulating and rewarding pastime. There are many different kinds of patchwork, and the following are three of the most popular. Mosaic, or 'English' patchwork is based on a simple repeated shape, such as a hexagon, diamond or square. Each separate patch is tacked over a paper template, and the patches are sewn together by hand.

Log Cabin patchwork does not require templates, and consists of strips of fabric sewn to a foundation in extending patterns of squares.

Machine or 'American' patchwork is based on a geometric pattern of divisions of a square. These squares are made up into larger areas forming intricate all-over patterns. The pattern units are put together by dressmaking methods. This type of patchwork, traditionally quilted is often termed 'American' patchwork although many of the designs originated in the north of England and were taken to America by settlers.

Mosaic or English Patchwork

This is the traditional method of tacking fabric over paper templates and then oversewing the covered shapes, or patches, into a pattern. This kind of patchwork is always done by hand.

Fabrics

Medium weight cottons are recommended for beginners. Always use the same type and weight of fabric in one article, i.e. all cotton, or all silk.

Thread

For tacking use mercerised cotton, which is finer than tacking cotton. For sewing the patches together use a fine cotton for cotton fabric, or silk for silk fabric. When sewing a dark patch to a lighter one, use dark thread.

Equipment

Templates These are the basic shapes required for cutting the lining papers and fabrics. They are often made from metal as they need to be hard-wearing, and must be accurately cut or the

Left: Hexagon Flower.
Right: "Baby Block" pattern.

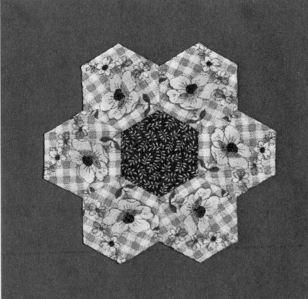

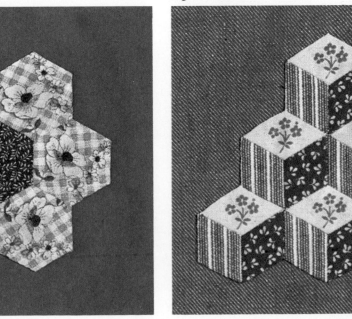

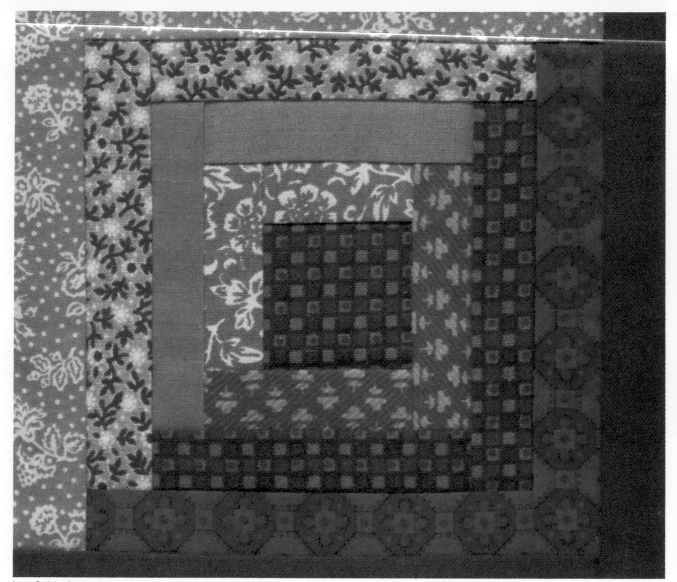

Log Cabin Square using cottons.

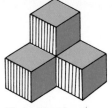

Diamonds in traditional 'baby block' pattern

patchwork will not fit together properly. Templates for short-term use can be cut from strong card.

Metal and Perspex templates can be purchased in various shapes and sizes from craft shops. They are measured by the length of one side. An easy shape to start with is the hexagon. Other popular shapes are the diamond, long hexagon, octagon, square, triangle and clamshell. The diagram shows some simple arrangements using hexagons and diamonds.

Hexagon rosette

A window template is a transparent version of the lining paper template, with an even 6mm (¼in) turning all round. It is used for accurate cutting of the patchwork fabric. When placed on the fabric the pattern can be outlined for accurate matching or perfect centring of motifs as shown.

Mosaic patchwork

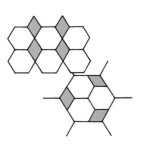

hexagons and diamonds

Lining paper Use fairly stiff paper such as bank or drawing paper, thin cards, pages from glossy

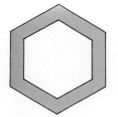

Window template

Transparent centre with 6mm turning allowance all round

Using window template to centre motif

magazines or unused brown paper.

You will also need fine steel pins, a pair of sharp long-bladed scissors for the fabric and an old pair of scissors for cutting the paper.

Design and Colour

Designs may use two or three templates, or may be based on a single template, but the final overall impression comes from the arrangement of tones (lightness and darkness) in the pattern.

Designs can be planned on graph paper and shaded in light, medium and dark tones, appropriate colours can then be chosen to suit the design. Alternatively a design can start from a collection of fabrics. For this method, make a number of patches (perhaps of hexagons, which are easy to fit together) and arrange them on the floor, or pin them to a board, until you find a pleasing pattern. Then stand back and see whether a light background would throw up the design or a dark one, and whether there is a sufficient amount of contrasting tone in the design.

A plain hexagon can be surrounded by six flowered ones, then this 'rosette' can be arranged with others on a background. A quiet colour scheme can be based on several shades of one colour, or a more lively one on contrasting colours, but remember to use dark, medium and light tones, whatever the colours may be.

Marking and Cutting Out

Cutting the paper The importance of accuracy when cutting the papers cannot be over-emphasised. The best method for cutting is to lay 3 or 4 layers of paper on a hard surface (such as a kitchen cutting board) with the template on top. Press down firmly and cut around with a craft knife.

An alternative method is to cut the paper with scissors, but this is less accurate and slower. Hold a piece of paper and the template firmly together in one hand, and cut cleanly across each side with the scissors pressed against the side of the template. Do not cut more than two at once, and do not draw round the template first as this will make the paper too big. If you wish to make half patches, cut the whole papers in half. Whichever method of cutting you use, remember that the papers form the base for each patch. Inaccurately cut papers will result in patches which are difficult, if not impossible, to sew together and will spoil the finished appearance of your work. Take as much trouble over cutting the papers as you possibly can as it will save time and even disappointment in the long run.

Cutting the fabric Cut the fabric using the window template. Lay the template on the fabric, pencil round it and cut out the shape. With practice, this process can be speeded up by holding the template and fabric together and cutting round

Tacking and Sewing the Patches

Tack the patches over the paper as follows and as shown in the accompanying diagrams:

(a) Pin the paper to the wrong side of the fabric, making sure the grain is in the right direction.

(b) Fold the fabric over at the corners as you work. Tack across the corners. Start with a knot, but do not fasten off, so that the stitches can easily be pulled out at the end.

Tacking the patches

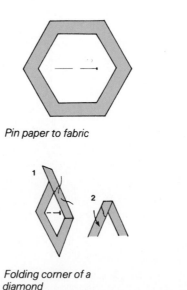

Pin paper to fabric

fold fabric over

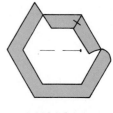

Folding corner of a diamond

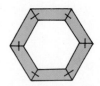

Fabric tacked over paper

Join the patches as follows: Hold two patches, right sides together, and oversew along the edge. Start a little way from one corner, work back to the beginning, work to the other corner, then work back a few stitches to fasten off. Take tiny stitches through the folds of the fabric, across the edge to be joined, but do not let the needle pierce the paper.

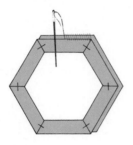

Sewing patches together

When the patchwork is complete, remove the tacking threads. Press lightly on the right side *before* taking out the papers, so that the turnings will not show as a line on the front.

Log Cabin Patchwork

This type of patchwork consists of strips of fabric sewn on to a square of foundation materials by hand or by machine. These patchwork squares can then be joined to form larger units. The size of the foundation square is variable, depending on the article being made, but is usually from 30cm to 38cm (12in to 15in) square for a bedcover and 15cm (6in) or less for cushion and small items.

Log Cabin Square using wools.

Colour

The pattern of Log Cabin relies on an arrangement of contrasting shades of fabrics. The traditional and effective result is obtained by using dark shades on two adjacent sides of a square and by using light shades on the remaining sides. Plain and patterned fabrics can be mixed — it is the colour tonal range that is important.

Fabrics

For the foundation fabric, choose a pre-shrunk calico or similar material. For the patchwork, the usual cottons and cotton blends are suitable, but thicker fabrics such a tweeds, woollen cloth and velvets and corduroy can also be used and even mixed in one piece of work.

To Make Log Cabin

If you are a beginner, we suggest working a trial square about 20cm (8in) finished size, with strips approximately 19mm (¾in) wide without turnings. The strips are cut to the width of a standard ruler, 3cm (1¼in), allowing 6mm (¼in) each side for turnings.

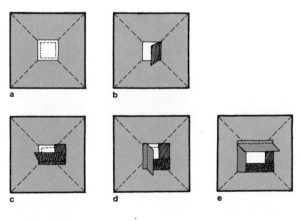

Log cabin patchwork

Marking and Cutting Out

Measure and cut out a 20cm (8in) square of foundation fabric, and draw pencil lines from corner to corner to determine the centre. Cut a 5cm (2in) square of fabric for the centre. Select fabrics in two distinct light and dark groupings, and using the width of a standard ruler as a guide, mark each side with pencil or dressmakers chalk and cut strips from each of the fabrics.

To Sew

Step 1 Place the small square on the foundation fabric, the corners meeting the drawn diagonal lines, and tack in place.

Step 2 Choosing a dark toned fabric, lay the first strip face down on the central square with the edges meeting, and cut the strip to the same length as the side of the square. Pin in place and taking a 6mm (¼in) seam allowance, sew with small running stitches or by machine. Fold the strip back over the stitches and press.

Step 3 Working in a clockwise direction and using the same fabric or one of similar tone, place the second strip along the next side of the square and cut so that it equals the side of the square plus the width of the first turned-back strip. Sew in place and turn back.

Step 4 Continue in this way round the square, the next two strips being of a lighter tone. Work a total of four rounds of strips, two dark fabrics and two light fabrics. When the fourth round of strips is folded back, the raw edges will meet those of the foundation fabric, and will be covered when the squares are joined together. The samples show finished squares ready for joining.

To finish the sample Line the square and finish with a bias trim of one of the fabrics used. This could be used as a mat, or pot holder.

To join squares Place two squares right sides together (take care to check the pattern shading is the correct way round) and sew together through all layers with a 6mm (¼in) seam.

Machine Patchwork

This type of work is sometimes called 'American patchwork. Three layers of fabric are used in this work. The top fabric is patchwork, the middle layer is padding of some kind, and the third layer forms the backing. These layers are sandwiched together and quilted through all three layers. The resulting fabric is highly decorative, strong and warm, making it ideal for clothing and quilts in particular.

The top fabric may be entirely patchwork, or may combine patchwork and appliqué, or consist entirely of applique. The latter is worked as described in the section on Appliqué.

The sewing techniques are simple, since they follow the usual dressmaking procedure of putting the right sides of the prepared fabric pieces together and seaming them with a straight machine or hand stitch.

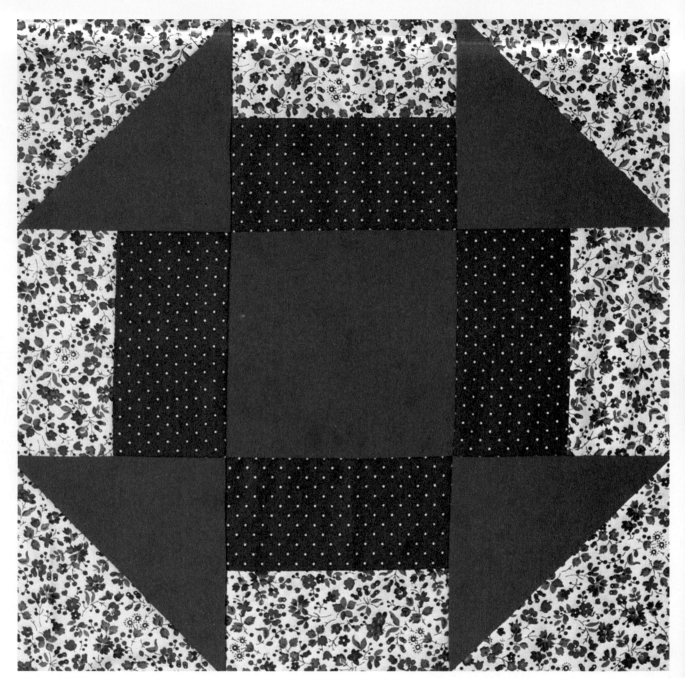

Sherman's March (sampler).

Fabrics

The top fabric should be pure cotton, polyester cotton mixture, or a similar fabric with a plain surface and a fairly firm weave. Try to buy fabric that is pre-shrunk, or wash it before starting work.

The padding can consist of thin wool or flannel, but the most useful kind is 2oz polyester wadding, sold by the metre. It is possible to buy large un-seamed pieces for quilts. If it is necessary to join wadding, lay the pieces side by side and work herringbone stitch across the join.

The backing fabric should be of the same weight and type as the top fabric, but avoid fabrics with a close weave as they are difficult to quilt. Sheeting makes an ideal backing for large pieces of work. Test all fabrics for colour fastness before starting work.

Threads

Use an ordinary sewing thread of the same type as your fabric, i.e. cotton with cotton. Match the colour to your fabric or choose the predominating colour, or a neutral shade like grey or beige.

For hand quilting use a strong, fine cotton or linen thread. Some specialist shops stock special quilting thread.

For machining, use No 40 mercerised cotton thread.

Design and Colour

Designs for this type of patchwork consist of geometric shapes which are divisions of a square. The squares are generally termed 'blocks'. Three examples of traditional block patterns are shown. When a number of these are joined, further patterns are formed, which is one of the fascinations of this type of design.

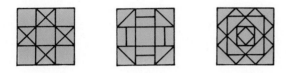

Colour is less important than tone, the lightness and darkness of the colour. The accompanying diagrams show the same block with six different arrangements of tones. You will note that the first diagram is all the same tone and therefore the pattern is lost.

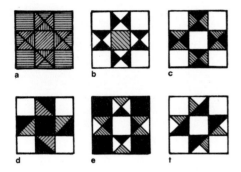

Making a Patchwork Block

The 'Shermans March' block, shown as a sample, is a good example of a 'three patch pattern'. That is to say, it is based upon three shapes, a triangle, a rectangle and a square. If you are a newcomer to patchwork, you might like to make this 'block', following the instructions below, as a practice piece. The finished size is approximately 30cm (12in) square, enough for a small item. Several squares could be joined together to make something larger.

Making the templates The pattern is based on a 10cm (4in) square. Draw three such squares on graph paper. Divide one vertically to make the rectangular template, and divide another diagonally to make the triangular template. Cut out the three shapes and stick them on thin card with 6mm (¼in) seam allowance all round.

To make your own block, draw it out full size on graph paper. Identify the different shapes and make templates as above.

Marking the fabric and cutting out Mark on the *wrong* side of the fabric. Draw round your card templates, holding the template firmly and keeping the line as close as possible to the edge of the template so that your patterns are not distorted.

A small piece of fine glass-paper glued to the back of a template will help to prevent it slipping.

Place the templates economically on the fabric. The straight side of your template should line up with the straight grain of the fabric. Cut out accurately on the lines you have drawn.

Sewing Place patches right sides together, matching the edges, pin and sew accurately 6mm (¼in) in from the edges as shown. Use a running stitch by hand, or a straight stitch by machine.

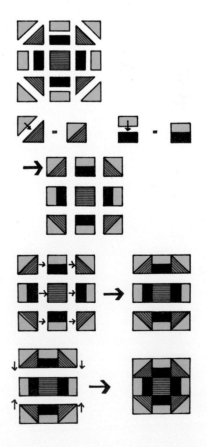

Sewing a complete block, 'Sherman's March'.

For hand-sewn seams draw a light pencil guide line. For machine-sewn seams use the presser foot for an accurate 6mm (¼in) allowance. Always work in easy units, simplifying the shapes you are working with. Sew together the patches for the Shermans March block following the plan given.

Pressing Press each seam to one side as soon as you have sewn it, so that it is accurately pressed open on the front, and flat on the back, before the complete piece is joined to the next. In general, press seams away from the centre, but modify this rule where pressing towards the centre will reduce the bulk of fabric, e.g. where seams cross. The reverse side of the Shermans March block is shown in the diagram.

Finally, press work on the *right* side to ensure seams are fully opened.

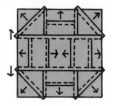

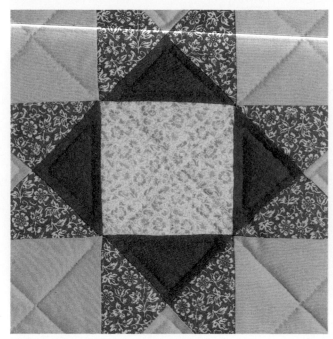

Variable Star.

Assembling the Layers for Quilting

Small projects can be tacked (basted) together and quilted without the use of a frame. The top, padding, and backing must be firmly tacked together without any folds or wrinkles. To do this, work on a flat surface such as a laminated table top. Fasten each layer in turn to the surface with bits of sticky tape all round, making sure that the fabric is smooth. Then tack through all layers in a grid pattern, working from the centre outwards. The quilting may then be worked in the hand.

Larger items can be mounted in a slate frame, as described in the first chapter. The backing is framed up, and the padding and the top fabric laid in position, pinned and then tacked as above. Quilting is worked in the frame.

Quilts are usually assembled and worked in a quilting frame. This need not be full size, as finished sections can be rolled round each end. Use two lengths of wood slightly wider than the quilt, and two as long as space will allow. Nail a strip of webbing to each length, and clamp the corners together. Support the frame at a convenient height using the backs of four chairs.

Each layer of the work is pinned or stitched to the webbing, and the tacking is worked from the centre outwards. Quilting by hand is worked in the frame. The work is taken off the frame if the quilting is worked by machine.

Quilting Patterns

The stitching patterns can be simple or complex, sometimes following the design of the patchwork, sometimes adding a new pattern. Some ideas are given in the accompanying diagram.

Mark your chosen pattern on the right side of the finished patchwork using a washable embroidery marker or a hard, well-sharpened pencil.

Marking outline quilting Traditionally the quilting stitches are placed 6mm (¼in) away from the seam lines, thus outlining the design. However, this can be varied — quilting should always please the eye.

Marking simple overall patterns Use a ruler or yardstick for straight lines, a plate or cup for repeated circular designs.

Marking more complex patterns Cut cardboard templates of the shapes in the chosen quilting design, and draw round them on the patchwork.

Quilting by hand The quilting stitch is a small, even running stitch. You can either take one or several stitches at a time, making sure that the needle passes through all layers.
Begin with a knot at the end of the thread. Insert the needle some distance away, and bring it out on the sewing line. Pull the thread, jerking the knot through the top fabric and burying it in the padding.
Finish by making a knot in your thread about 2.5cm (1in) from the last stitch. Insert the needle in the sewing line again, and emerge some distance away. Jerk the thread so that the knot disappears into the padding. Snip the thread off close to the fabric. In this way there is no apparent break in the quilting lines.

Quilting by machine If you are quilting a large item, make sure it will pass under the arm of your machine. If not, it will have to be worked in several sections.

Tack the work firmly as described, and machine along the quilting lines you have drawn, using a stitch suited to the thickness of the fabrics. Begin and end each line of quilting with a few back stitches. Finish the edges by any of the methods suggested in the section on Quilting.

Martha Washington Star.

QUILTING

Quilting is a decorative method of stitching layers of fabric together, enclosing a filling, to produce a raised surface pattern. It is a very old technique, and was much used in the past to make warm bedclothing and garments. Today quilting is still used for warmth, but there is a lot more variety in fillings and quilting techniques.

There are four basic types of quilting, called Wadded (or English), Corded (or Italian), Stuffed (or Trapunto) and Shadow quilting. Each technique uses the same simple stitches to sew together two or more layers of fabric, but the variations in design, fabrics and fillings produce widely differing results.

Wadded Quilting

This is also known as English quilting. Wadded quilting is primarily used for warmth, and consists of a filling sandwiched between two layers of fabric, all three layers being stitched together in an all-over design.

Materials

Top A plain pale fabric with a slight sheen shows up a quilting pattern best. Silk, cotton, fine linen or thin wool are all suitable, and chamois leather and suede can also be used. Many man-made fibres are too springy for quilting, but those which include a percentage of natural fibre are acceptable.

Patterned fabric can be used for contour quilting. Choose an all-over pattern of simple shapes, in proportion to the project. That is to say, you could use a large pattern for a quilt, but a small print would be more suitable for a cushion.

Filling Synthetic wadding made especially for quilting can be bought in various weights. This comes either by the metre, or in single or double bed sizes for quilts. Traditionally, quilts were filled with old blankets, or teased-out sheep's wool. These can still be used, but synthetic wadding has the advantage of being light and easily washable. Other suggested fillings are a proprietary brand of a loosely-knitted interlining fabric, flannel, flannelette, and thin woollens. Felt, foam and cotton wool do not wear well.

Backing If the article is to be reversible then the backing should be the same as the top fabric. Otherwise a plainer and cheaper fabric, such as soft cotton, can be used. Where the backing will be concealed by a lining, as in a garment, it can be of muslin or cheesecloth.

Threads Match the thread to the colour and fibre of the top fabric. For cotton, use sewing cotton 40

Wadded quilting.

Contour quilting.

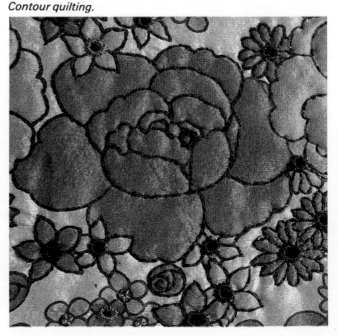

or 50, or buttonhole twist. For silk, use silk thread. For wool, use either cotton or silk. A specially strong quilting cotton can be bought for use on cotton or linen.

Needles Use the short betweens needles, average size 8.

Frame Small items can be worked in the hand or mounted in a ring frame as described on page 5. Larger items can be mounted in a slate frame as described on page 5. Quilts which are to be worked in the hand, can be tacked together and then worked in a special quilting frame in sections. The backing can be stapled to a home-made frame (page 6) and the filling and top fabric spread over and tacked (basted) in place.

Design

The traditional design for wadded quilting is an all-over pattern, often with borders, built up with the repeated use of simple templates. In the past the latter were household objects such as cups, saucers and wine glasses. The one essential for a wadded quilting design is that the stitching should cover the whole area, through all three layers, bonding them permanently into place.

Designs can be regular and geometric (as shown in the sample, using a coin and a square of card for templates), or rounded and flowing like the cable border shown in the diagram, which is built up from a single template. Contour quilting consists simply of quilting round the outlines of a patterned fabric — or alternatively, the outlines are worked round applied shapes.

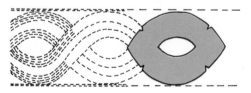

Cable border with template

Transferring the Design It is difficult to use transfers or pencil lines for marking out quilting designs without them showing through or smudging. The recommended methods are Trace and tack, or Needlemarking round templates.

Trace and tack The design should be traced and tacked on the top fabric before the three layers are put together.

Needlemark method This is used on the top fabric when all three layers have been tacked together, and framed up if necessary. Start from the centre and work outwards. Place the template in posi-

tion on the top fabric. Holding a needle at an angle, mark firmly round the shape. Remove the template. The indented line should remain long enough to be worked.

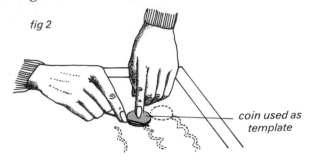

fig 2 — coin used as template

Needlemarking

Preparing the Fabric

Iron both the top and backing fabric. On the top fabric, mark the centre lines on the grain of the fabric both vertically and horizontally by tacking or chalk marks. Also mark the diagonals, the position of the corners and the width of any borders. Transfer the design if using Trace and Tack method. Frame up if required, or lay the three fabrics together and tack firmly all over.

Tacking Thorough tacking is essential for a good piece of quilting. This can be done on a frame as shown in the diagram or by hand. Firmly tack the top, wadding and backing together. Make sure that there are no folds or wrinkles by working on a flat table-top. You can fasten down the layers with adhesive tape. Work from the centre outwards, tacking through all the layers in a grid pattern.

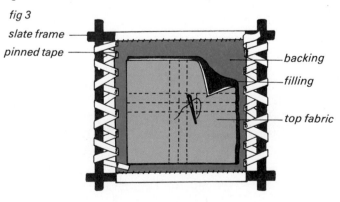

fig 3 — slate frame — pinned tape — backing — filling — top fabric

Tacking (basting)

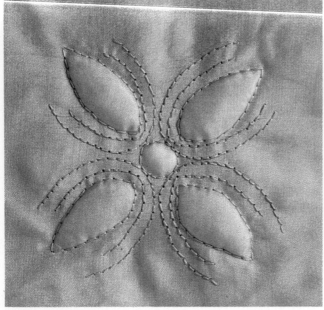

Stuffed quilting.

point where it first came through. Work small even stitches, and make sure that the needle passes vertically through the three fabrics each time, never at an angle.

Chain stitch Chain stitch makes a bolder outline, and is often worked in heavier thread than running and back stitch. The method of working is shown on page 9. The back of the work will show a row of straight stitches. This method is not recommended for well padded pieces of work, as the needle tends to go in at an angle, and the stitch does not hold the three layers together as firmly as running or back stitch.

Straight stitch by machine Use a fairly long stitch, and set the tension so that the stitch lock comes right in the middle of the wadding. It is difficult to machine large items without puckering the backing fabric.

Embroidery Stitches such as satin stitch, stem stitch, eyelets and French knots (see Stitches Section), can be used to decorate quilting designs.

Finishing off Quilting looks well with a simple finish. Three different edge treatments are shown in the diagram.

Stitches

Running stitch This is the traditional quilting stitch and should be worked as evenly as possible, each stitch going right through three layers every time the needle passes. The best method of ensuring this is to work the stitch in two movements. This stitch will look the same on both sides of the work.

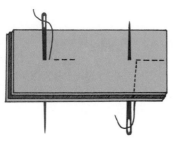

Running stitch

Back stitch This stitch is also best worked in two movements. It makes a very firm line, but should only be used on pieces where the back will not be seen. Bring the needle up on the stitch line. Insert the needle again a small distance behind this, pull it through to the back, then bring it up the same distance in front. Insert the needle again at the

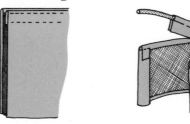

Quilting stitch hem   *Piped hem*

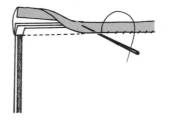

Bound hem

Corded Quilting

This method is also called Italian quilting. Corded quilting is decorative rather than warm. Only two layers of fabric are used, a good top fabric and a thinner backing fabric. The design is outlined with parallel lines of stitchery, and when the

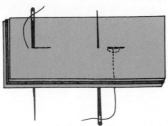

Backstitch

work is complete these channels are threaded with thick yarn from the back, making the design stand out in relief on the front.

Materials

Top The same type of fabric can be used as for Wadded quilting, as well as heavier and richer fabrics.

Filling The channels are threaded with one or more strands of thick yarn. There is a special quilting yarn made for the purpose, or you can use knitting wools, rug yarn or cotton cords such as candlewick and piping cord. If the top fabric is leather, hard cord or string will make the design stand out.

Backing As this is not generally seen, it can be of cheaper and lighter fabric. Muslin and organdie are often used, partly because they can easily be pierced by the blunt needle used for threading the channels, and partly because they are semi-transparent, and the design can be traced off and worked from the back.

Threads As for Wadded quilting.

Needles As for Wadded quilting.

Frame Small pieces can be worked in the hand, or in a hoop frame. Larger pieces should be framed up to prevent puckering, on either a slate frame or a home-made frame.

Design

Corded quilting designs consist of lines rather than shapes, and simple curving or interlacing patterns are the most suitable. Aim for long continuous lines without sharp curves, as this makes it easier to thread the channels.

Stuffed and corded quilting.

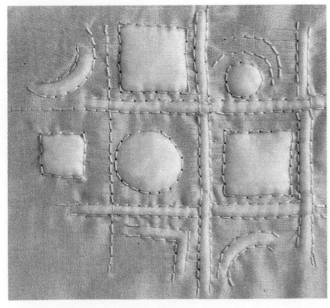

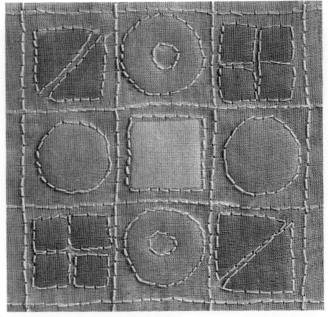

Shadow wadded quilting using felt.

Transferring the design This can be done by the Trace and Tack method on the front (page 67), or by using Muslin Transfer on the back.

Muslin transfer Lay the piece of muslin or organdie used for backing over the design. Fix it so that it will not move, and trace off the design on to the muslin with a pen or pencil. This backing and the top fabric are then tacked together, and the design is worked from the back.

Preparing the Fabric

Iron the top and backing fabric. Mark centre lines and trace off the design on to either the top or bottom fabric as desired. Frame up if necessary.

Tacking As for Wadded Quilting.

Stitches

Working from the front, use back stitch, running stitch or chain stitch.

Working from the back with a muslin transfer, use a small running stitch. Straight stitch by machine is successful with this method and gives a nice sharp outline to the design. This can be worked either from the front or the back.

Threading the channels When the stitching is finished, turn the work to the back. Use a short blunt needle with a large enough eye to take the chosen quilting yarn. Insert the needle through the backing into the beginning of a channel. Come out about half a needle-length further on, pulling the yarn evenly along the channel behind. Re-insert the needle in the same hole and bring it out a little further on, pulling the yarn almost all the way through, but leaving a tiny loop at each opening. This allowance will be taken up in wash and wear and prevents the fabric puckering. Work in short needle lengths, coming out of the channel at regular intervals, and more often round curves and corners. Where the channels cross, bring the yarn out of the underneath one and re-insert it beyond the crossing line.

Finishing off As for Wadded Quilting.

Corded quilting. Threading the channels

Stuffed Quilting

Stuffed quilting or Trapunto is a purely decorative method of quilting which uses two layers of fabric. The design is outlined in stitchery, and certain areas are padded from the back, so that they stand out on the top fabric.

Materials

Top Fabric This should have the same qualities as those described for Wadded quilting, that is to say, a slight sheen and a gentle pliability. It is possible to use knitted fabrics if they are not too loose in texture.
Filling This can be odd lengths of quilting yarn, or scraps of synthetic wadding, or best of all, natural wool which is washed and ready for use. This can be bought at the chemist under the name of Chiropody Wool. Kapok and cotton wool are not recommended for practical items as they become lumpy.
Backing This should be firm and closely woven, such as strong cotton or calico or best quality organdie. If the backing is too soft, the padding will be raised up on the back of the work rather than on the front.
Threads As for Wadded Quilting.
Needles As for Wadded Quilting.
Frame Designs for stuffed quilting are best worked in a frame, which prevents puckering when the back of the work is stuffed. Frame up as described on page 67.

Design

Only selected areas of the design are padded. These should be kept small, as large areas of padding over weight the fabric. Keep to simple outlines, as it is difficult to stuff complicated shapes. Stuffed quilting is usually combined with other kinds of quilting or embroidery.

Transferring the Design This can be done by the Trace and Tack method on the top fabric, or by the muslin transfer method on the backing fabric. If the backing fabric is not transparent, the design can be ironed off on to it by transfer sheet or pencil, and the piece worked from the back.

Preparing the Fabric

Iron, mark and frame up if necessary as for Wadded Quilting.

Tacking Tack both fabrics together as described for Wadded Quilting.

Stitches The same as for Corded Quilting.

Stuffing When the design has all been stitched, turn the work over to the back and stuff the selected areas as follows:- Cut a little slit in the middle of the area to be stuffed. Poke in bits of yarn or wadding with a knitting needle or orange stick, until the space is comfortably full. Stitch up the slit, being careful not to pull too tightly.

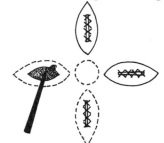

Trapunto quilting. Stuffing the shapes from the back

Shadow Quilting

All the foregoing kinds of quilting can be turned into 'Shadow' quilting by the use of see-through top fabrics and coloured fillings. Use thin semi-transparent fabrics for the top such as Jap silk, chiffon, georgette and organdie, and stuff with coloured wadding or yarns.

Instead of wadding, pieces of brightly coloured felt or vilene can be sandwiched between two layers of semi-transparent fabric. The coloured shapes are laid in position and outlined in stitches worked through both the top and bottom fabric.

APPLIQUE

Appliqué is the art of applying one fabric to another, by hand or machine stitchery, with or without added embroidery. It is one of the quickest and easiest kinds of needlecraft, creating a rewarding effect with a minimum of sewing. It is a very adaptable technique which can be used for many kinds of practical and decorative projects.

Modern embroidered panels use a great deal of applique. In these, scraps of every kind of fabric, from leather to organdie, are applied to a background to achieve a dramatic pictorial effect. In a simpler way, delicate sprays of flowers or motifs can be applied to lingerie or baby-wear.

Motifs applied with a sewing machine provide a quick and easy way of decorating garments and quilts and this kind of applied work will stand up well to hard wear and washing.

Depending on the type of applique you wish to do, there is a wide choice of different fabrics and techniques.

Choice of Fabrics

A firm, closely woven fabric of medium weight is best for backgrounds. Avoid fabrics that stretch or fray. The easiest fabrics to apply are felt, leather and other non-woven fabrics. However, by using special iron-on nylon bonding webs most fabrics can be made non-fraying nowadays with a little advance preparation.

For practical items, choose colourfast and washable fabrics, and make sure that the applied pieces and the background fabric are the same weight — that is to say, apply cotton on cotton, wool on wool.

For panels, all kinds of fabrics can be used and it is interesting to experiment with layers of transparent fabrics, and to alter the applied fabric by withdrawing threads, folding and pleating it, or applying it gathered or bunched up.

Traditional appliqué with turnings.

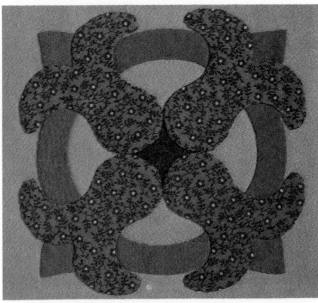

Threads

For practical items and for machine stitching, use cotton or silk threads for natural fibres, and synthetic thread for man-made fibres. It helps to unify a design if different shapes and colours are all applied with the same colour of thread. In general, the thread should be unobtrusive, when used for the actual appliqué, although all kinds of threads may be used for added embroidery.

Edge Treatment

This should be considered at the design stage. Edges can be treated so that the stitchery is invisible, they can be machined over to make a strong line, or embroidered over so that the edge shades off into the background. Each method gives a different emphasis to the design as illustrated by the samples in this section, each of which shows a different edge treatment.

Designs

Appliqué design is based on bold and simple shapes. As a start, one or two repeating shapes can be arranged in a pleasing pattern on the background. Designs can be based on folded paper cut-outs, simple geometric shapes like circles and squares, abstract motifs, or natural ones like sprays of flowers. The shapes can be arranged symmetrically, singly or overlapped.

Transferring Designs

Whole designs can be transferred to the background fabric by any of the methods described in the first chapter. Alternatively, if only a few simple shapes are involved, these can be cut out and positioned directly on the background.

The design motifs can also be transferred by several different methods. Card templates may be used, or tracing through dressmakers' carbon, or applying directly with the Trace, Pin and Sew method.

To make a template Trace or draw a separate motif for each part of the design you wish to apply on thick paper or thin card using carbon paper to help you. Remember to include any markings, such as stitching lines.

Cut out the traced shape which is then called a 'template' and identify the back and front of the template. No allowance for turnings is included on card templates as a rule.

Methods of Work

Basically, there are three different ways of working simple appliqué. Firstly, there is the traditional method, whereby the background fabric is framed up, the applied pieces are cut, (with turnings if the fabric is frayable) and the pieces pinned, tacked and sewn in place.

Secondly, there is the quick and easy no-sew method, using one of the special bonding webs. This material is sold in small packs and can be obtained from haberdashery sections of department stores and fabric retailers. Here, the design motifs are ironed straight on to the background.

Thirdly, there is the Trace, Pin and Sew method, where the fabric to be applied is stitched to the background by machine through a tracing of the design.

Preparation of background fabric Always iron the fabric before starting work. Then, using chalk lines or a row of pins or tacking, mark centre lines on the fabric from top to bottom and side to side. Use these marks to position the design tracing or templates.

Traditional Method

This is worked in a frame. Prepare the fabrics and frame up the background fabric in a ring, slate or home-made frame as described in the first chapter. Lay the template, or trace the design, on the applied fabric in such a way that when the motif is laid on the background the grain direction of both fabrics will match. Unless the fabric is a non-woven one, remember to add a 6mm (¼in) seam allowance all round. Cut the design motifs out.

Tack the seam allowance under on each motif before the piece is applied to the background. On

Traditional appliqué without turnings.

curved sections, cut V-shaped notches almost to the stitching line before turning the seam allowance under. At the corners, snip straight across just outside the seam line, turn under a tiny hem, then fold in the sides along the seam line and tack.

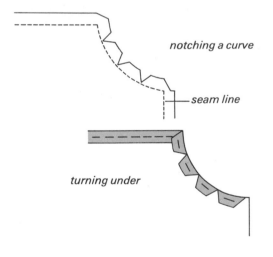

notching a curve

seam line

turning under

Tacking under a seam allowance

Pressing is optional — a pressed edge will look flat and sharp, while an unpressed edge will look slightly raised.

Pin prepared motifs in position on the background fabric, matching grain of fabrics, and using fine steel pins placed at right angles to the edges of the motifs. If the motif is large, tack it in place both horizontally and vertically, working from the centre. Never tack round the edge.

Using matching thread and a fine needle, stab stitch all round the edge as invisibly as possible. This edge is often embroidered over afterwards.

Appliqué using the no-sew method.

Appliqué using the trace, pin and sew method.

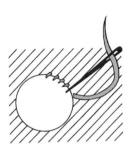

Stab stitch

No-Sew Method

First back a piece of the fabric to be applied with pieces of an adhesive nylon web, following the manufacturer's instructions. Then mark and cut out the motif using method (a), (b) or (c) below.

(a) Pencil round a reversed template of the motif on the paper backing. Cut along pencilled line.

(b) Lay a template of the motif right way up on the right side of the fabric. Hold motif and fabric firmly together and cut out round the template.

(c) Trace round a template of the design motif through dressmakers' carbon paper on the right side of the fabric and cut out.

Peel off the backing paper. Position the motif on the prepared background material and iron in place following the manufacturer's instructions.

Trace, Pin and Sew

Make a tracing of the design motif on greaseproof or tracing paper. Cut out, leaving a 2.5cm (1in) border all round.

Lay the piece of fabric to be applied on the prepared background matching the grain of the fabrics. Lay the tracing in position on top. Put

pins in all round at right angles to the outline. Machine round the outline. Take out the pins. Tear off the tracing. Trim fabric close to the stitched outline. Hand embroider or machine zig-zag over the raw edge.

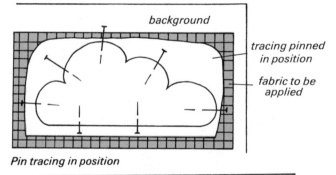

Pin tracing in position

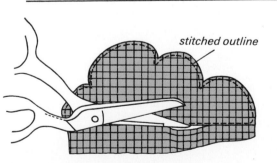

Stitch round. Tear off tracing. Trim away surplus fabric

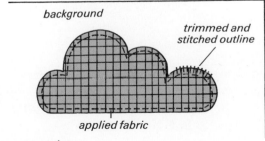

Zig-zag over edge

FINISHING OFF

Stretching

Stretching is a method of making a piece of work smooth and flat and at the same time squaring it up. This is particularly important with canvas work, which tends to become distorted as the work progresses. Work carried out on a frame can be stretched on the frame, but work done in the hand or in small ring frames will need stretching on a board.

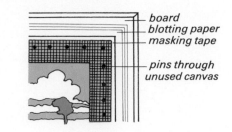

stretching canvas

Stretching on the frame

1 Check that the fabric will not mark with water.
2 Dampen the work all over the back with a well-wrung sponge.
3 Tighten the frame, making sure that all the corners are at right angles.
4 Leave to dry at room temperature before taking it off the frame.

Stretching on a board

1 Check that your fabric will not mark with water.
2 If there is not enough margin of background fabric to pin out the embroidery, stitch a strip round the outer edge.
3 Lay several sheets of clean, wet blotting paper, larger than the embroidery, on a board which will take drawing pins. Drain off the excess water.
4 Lay the embroidery face up on the blotting paper. If canvas work is being stretched, dampen the wrong side with a squeezed sponge.

6 Check the measurements of the width and height, and find the position of the bottom right corner and mark it. Pin from the sides already in place to that corner. Make sure all the sides are at right angles.
7 Leave at room temperature until it is thoroughly dry before taking it off the board.

Pressing

Never put an iron on the right side of a piece of embroidery. Even on the wrong side use a pressing cloth between the work and the iron.
1 Lay a folded cloth or two on the ironing board.
2 Lay the embroidery face down on the cloth.
3 Cover with a pressing cloth (wet or dry depending on the type of fabric to be ironed), and press gently all over with the iron at the correct heat.
4 Leave to dry flat at room temperature.

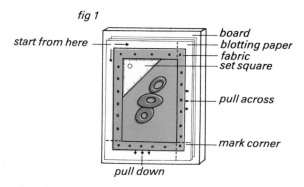

Stretching fabric

5 Stretch and pin straight across the top of the embroidery, keeping the drawing pins outside the actual area of the work. Using a set square, or corner of card that has a right angle, align the edge at the left side and pin in place.

Mounting

Panels which are to be hung up should first be mounted over heavy card or softboard as follows:
1 Run a tacking thread round the outer edge of the embroidery so that the size can be calculated.
2 Cut strong card or board to the size of the work. Make sure the sides are at right angles.
3 If no further mounting is considered, you will need a hanging cord. Make two holes through the board, as shown, and thread a thin flat ribbon through. Tie on the back.
4 Lay the embroidery face down on a flat surface and centre the board on the back. Fold the fabric back all round and, using a firm thread or fine string, lace the opposite sides back and forth every inch or so. Tighten when the end is reached and finish off. Repeat in the opposite direction,

trim the corners and stitch down. Press these corners with a damp cloth if they do not seem flat enough.

5 Alternatively, glue or staple the fabric to the back of the board.

6 Round panels can be mounted on cake boards, if you can find one the right size. In this case the fabric can be glued or stapled to the back.

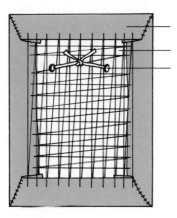

Mounting a panel

Ideas for Framing

Use of a Conventional Frame Generally, with embroidered work, the plainer the frame, the better the work will be displayed. You can use plain wooden or gold and silver frames. Conventional frames look best with work that has plenty of background fabric showing, and which is not very heavy or woolly in nature. The embroidery should be stretched over thin board (make sure the corners are exact right angles), and fixed in the frame in the usual way with panel pins. Glass is not generally needed with embroidery — surprisingly enough the work does not seem to get dirty. A hanging cord can be stretched across the sides of the frame, held with screws with a ring.

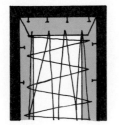

Framing a mounted panel

Card Mount A card mount would be used when the embroidery is small, fine and fairly flat. It is laid over the stretched and mounted embroidery. Any kind of mount will extend the area round the

embroidery, creating a smooth expanse before the final framing or edging. The colour of the mount should complement the fabric and the embroidery. The frame can be a contrast, or can blend with the mount. The latter will set off the embroidery to greater effect.

Decide on the size and shape of the area to be cut out by laying four strips of paper round the design and moving them about until a satisfactory effect is achieved. Measure the aperture. When cutting out remember to make the depth of the mount at the bottom, greater than that at the top, as this gives a more balanced look.

Equipment You will need a craft knife, a steel rule, adhesive tape and a soft pencil. Choose a piece of mounting card in a suitable colour and of the required size. For a straight sided mount proceed as follows:

1 Lay the card face upwards on a surface that can be scored with a knife.

2 Rule the lines to be cut with a pencil, starting at the bottom with a line parallel to the lower edge. Then use a set square for the two sides. Extend the lines to form a cross in the corners.

3 Working from the corners into the centre of each side, score the knife along lightly three or four times until there is a groove to guide the knife, then make a clean cut along the length.

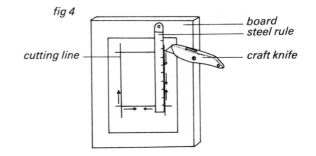

Cutting a card mount

Fabric Mount Fabric mounts are made by covering card mounts with fabric. They differ from card mounts in that you are adding a texture as well as a colour. The fabric should be thinnish so that it will fold over the mount easily, and it is best to choose a colour that is already in the embroidery (your eye links the two together and the mount becomes an extension of the embroidery). Use a fabric mount where there is a lot of concentrated stitchery. It helps to emphasise the textile nature of an embroidery.

To cover a card mount with fabric
1 Work on a soft board that will take pins.

2 Lay the fabric face down. Lay the cut-out card mount in the centre.

3 Pin the card mount to the board through the fabric, at 2.5cm (1in) intervals, with steel pins.

4 Cut out the fabric centre leaving a 19mm (¾in) border all round the inside of the card mount.

5 Cut into each corner of inner fabric border, stopping fractionally short of the card. Turn back the fabric edges and glue them to the card mount.

6 To complete the inner corners, put a spot of glue on each inner card corner, press each corner of the fabric up against the glued card, and hold with a pin as shown. Leave to dry.

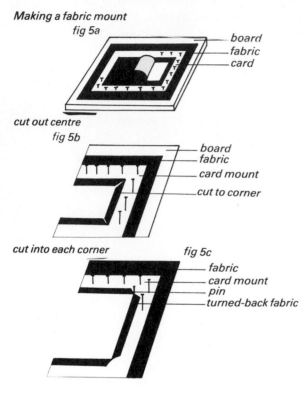

Making a fabric mount
fig 5a

— board
— fabric
— card

cut out centre
fig 5b

— board
— fabric
— card mount
— cut to corner

cut into each corner   *fig 5c*

— fabric
— card mount
— pin
— turned-back fabric

turn back edges, push pin in corner

7 Unpin, turn fabric-covered mount over and position it on the embroidery. Fold the outer edges of the fabric over both the card and the mounted embroidery and glue or staple to the back.

Positioning a mount

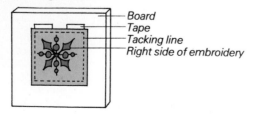

— Board
— Tape
— Tacking line
— Right side of embroidery

Lay strips of tape under top edge of embroidery

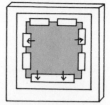

Lay card mount in position and press to tape   *Turn over. Tape all round*

Flat Mount This is a flat piece of board, larger and often thicker than the mounted embroidery, which is secured to the back of the work with four screws. Glue can be used for light pieces, but is not so reliable.

This flat mount can be covered with fabric or with paper, wallpaper, cork tiles or other textured materials. Attach the embroidery (mounted on card or board) to this background as shown.

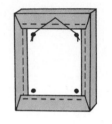

A flat mount
a) Clamp boards together and screw through into smaller one
b) Tie hanging cord to the two top screws
c) Front view. Smaller board edged with velvet ribbon

Finishing off a home-made frame If the home-made frame has been covered carefully it may need no further attention. If however the edges are a bit rough, they can be covered with either velvet ribbon, or strips of wood.

Edging home-made frames

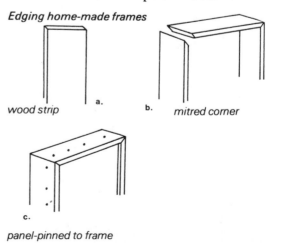

wood strip   *a.*   *b.*   *mitred corner*

panel-pinned to frame

Velvet Ribbon Edging Use the same width as the thickness of the mount if possible. If not, use a slightly wider ribbon, keep the front edge flush with the mount and turn in the extra at the back and glue it in place. Use a PVA glue.

Wood Strip Edging Use strips of natural wood, available from DIY shops, from 3mm to 6mm (1/8in to ¼in) thick, wide enough to cover the edge of the mount and stand proud of the embroidery by about 6mm (¼in). Cut as for a picture frame and mitre the corners. These need not be glued to each other, but just fitted closely round the edge of the frame, and panel pinned.

Greetings Cards A small neat piece of embroidery makes a good greetings card. Use thin card for this, and stiff paper for the inner folds, and work as follows:

(a) The card should extend at least 2.5cm (1in) beyond the embroidery, with a slightly larger allowance on the lower edge. Decide how the card is to fold, and cut a piece of card the full size. Cut an opening in the front as for the card mount, in a shape to suit the design.

(b) Tape the embroidery in place, check it is in the right position, then finish gluing or taping all round. Make sure the fabric extends at least 12mm (½in) beyond the edges of the opening.

(c) Couch a smooth thread round the embroidery on the very edge of the opening.

(d) Cut a piece of paper 3mm (1/8in) smaller all round than the finished card. Fold it in half, insert it in the card and glue one half around the back of the embroidery (not *on* it). The other half of the paper forms a sheet on which to write.

Greetings cards

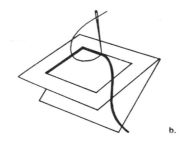

Square and rectangular cards

Couching a thread round the edge

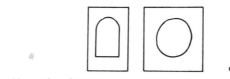

Alternative shapes

A sample of smocking in Honeycomb stitch, row 1: Stem; row 2: rows of Honeycomb, (See Smocking pages 42–47).

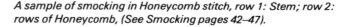

USEFUL INFORMATION

Needle sizes for single-thread canvas

Holes per inch	Needle sizes
24	24
22	22
20	22
18	22
16	22
14	20
10	18/20

Needle sizes for double-thread canvas

Holes per inch	Needle sizes
11	20
10	18
5	13/14
3	12

Metric Conversions

1 in	25.4 mm
1 ft	0.3048 m
1 yd	0.9144 m
1 sq in	6.4516 sq cm
1 sq ft	0.092903 sq m
1 cm	0.3937 in
1 m	3.280839 ft
1 m	1.09361 yd
1 sq cm	0.155 sq in
1 sq m	1.19599 sq yd

USA and Canada

In the United States and Canada Anchor Stranded Cotton is Embroidery Floss and Anchor Tapisserie Wool is Tapestry Wool.

Bibliography

A World of Embroidery, Mary Gostelow, Mills & Boon, 1975

Appliqué, Evangeline Shears and Diantha Fielding, Pan Books, 1972.

Bargello Stitchery, Jo Ippolito Christensen and Sonie Shapiro Ashner, Sterling Publishing Company, 1972.

Embroidery and Colour, Constance Howard, Batsford, 1976.

Good Housekeeping Step-by-Step Encyclopedia of Needlecraft, Judy Brittain, Ebury Press, 1979.

Patchwork Quilts, Averil Colby, Batsford, 1965

Smocking in Embroidery, Margaret Thom, Batsford, 1972.

The Book of Creative Crafts, edited by Elsie Burch Donald, Octopus, 1978.

INDEX